HOW TO ENJOY A
Good Life with Your Teenager

ANGELA BARRON McBRIDE, PH.D.

GW00708121

FISHER BOOKS

Publisher   Bill Fisher
             Helen Fisher
             Howard W. Fisher
             Tom Monroe, P.E.

Cover Design: Josh Young
Book Design: Jesica Shatan

Published by Fisher Books
P.O. Box 38040
Tucson, AZ 85740-8040
602/292-9080

Library of Congress Cataloging-in-Publication Data

McBride, Angela Barron.
  [Secret of a good life with your teenager]
  A good life with your teenager /
Angela Barron McBride.
  p. cm.
Originally published: The secret of a good life with your teenager.
1st ed. New York, N.Y.: Times Books, ©1987.
Bibliography: p.

  1. Adolescence. 2. Parenting. 3. Conflict of generations. I. Title
HQ796.M384 1989
305.23'5--d20   89-7714
ISBN 1-55561-023-4

Printed in U.S.A.
Printing 10 9 8 7 6 5 4 3

Notice: The information in this book is true and complete to the best of our knowledge. It is offered with no guarantees on the part of the author or Fisher Books. The author and publisher disclaim all liability in connection with use of this book.

• CONTENTS •

• FOR MY DAUGHTERS, CAMMIE AND KARA •

Child of mine, miniature me,
Reaching out, but shadow close;
We play and dance together—
In step, following my lead.

Child of mine, beyond my reach,
The high-noon sun burns the link.
We head for separate shade;
Each whole, each missing a piece.

Child of mine, I lean on you.
I have become your shadow.
Will you try to run from me?
Will you stay with me 'til night?

—A.B.McB.

· ACKNOWLEDGMENTS ·

My experience as a Kellogg National Fellow between 1981 and 1984 prompted the writing of this book. My project on "Stages of Parenting" involved an extensive review of the parenting literature, conducting a series of formal interviews with parents of teenagers, and the opportunity for ample interdisciplinary discussion of these issues. I am grateful to Elizabeth Grossman, Dean of the Indiana University School of Nursing, for expediting the sabbatical leave that allowed me to have time to weave together the experiences of those years.

I am indebted to Elisabeth Scharlatt, Susan Lescher, Kathryn Norcross Black, Lucy McGough, Jacqueline Fogel, and Patricia Welch for their help in clarifying my thinking. Judy Yost provided me with support services that facilitated my writing.

Loving thanks to Bill McBride for many hours of helpful editorial consultation, and to my daughters Cammie and Kara for teaching me so much about the subject matter. Finally, I would like to express my appreciation to all the parents who generously shared their thoughts and feelings, and to Jane M. Kirschling, who conducted some of these interviews.

· INTRODUCTION ·

I will never forget my first outing as a new mother. Twice, someone came over to congratulate me and ended by saying, "Enjoy her now, because you'll feel quite the opposite when she's a teenager." It felt as if the bad witch in Sleeping Beauty had come to my party and wished me an evil that would surely overtake me, no matter what I did to stop it. I was having some difficulty adjusting to being a mother, and I felt as if everyone were saying there is nowhere to go but down. No amount of rationalizing about the fact that what people say indicates more about them than about me, touched my distress. The teenage years seemed destined to be awful!

My experience is far from unique. In the Western world, the teenage years have both an awesome and awful reputation. Parents are regularly warned, "Just you wait." You feel cursed; this sweet infant will self-destruct come the teenage years in an explosion of sex, drugs, violence, venereal disease, and drunken driving while sporting a dirty punk hairdo and screaming obscenities. I once talked with a new mother who proudly showed me her firstborn son, then wondered aloud if he would be dealing dope and hating her by the time he was sixteen. She dreaded what the future held, though this was a time of promise and beginnings.

Some of the fear that present parents have about the teenage years may be due to the fact that the baby-boom generation, one-third of our present population, collectively had such a sensationally exhibitionistic adolescence that they gave all subsequent teenagers a bad reputation. The number of teenagers in the United States, which had dropped by 1.5 million in the late 1940s to 10 million, doubled by 1970 and hit 20 million. Positive parts of the experience may have been glossed over because the worst elements of the collective image were so noticeable. Being a teenager seemed to be synonymous with depravity and protest. Landon Jones describes the baby boomers during their teenage years as "a critical mass of teenagers that was as fissionable as any nuclear pile."[1] The seemingly explosive nature of teenagers of that generation was an artifact of numbers rather than an intrinsic quality of adolescence, but the spirit of dread lives on into present times.

Parents worry about what their experience will be when their children are teenagers. Is the bad press teenagers have at all true? Will their children experiment the way they did? Will all the surliness and ingratitude that they once heaped upon their parents come back to haunt them? Will the known and loved child become a despised unknown? What to expect is not clear, so many parents dread the worst. Parents are concerned that they will not be up to the requirements of the task ahead. Will they be able to handle all the rapid changes of that time? Are they prepared for the second decade of parenthood?

It is true that something new happens about the time your child reaches double-digit status. You become amazed that the child is growing up so fast. The soft, sweet, cuddly, and fluffy images that you equated with childhood no longer hold. Sometimes, the child's reality seems very removed from your dream child:

It was difficult for Tom to realize that his son was ten years old now. The child he conjured up when he closed his eyes at night was always an infant, the tangled hair still as smooth as peach fuzz, with the scars and bruises of summer erased, so that Byron was again a sleek, seal-like baby.[2]

There is someone new living with you, someone you are unprepared to deal with since the overwhelming majority of all discussions about childrearing center on the transition to parenthood and the child's early years.

It is not as if the years since the child's birth have been uniformly full of pastel-colored feelings. Maybe you had a difficult time adjusting to the demand feeding of a demanding infant. Maybe toilet training was a nasty clash of wills. Maybe the child took a long time to get adjusted to a school routine. But no matter what problems you experienced in the first decade of parenthood, you usually reach the end of that period in a relatively rosy frame of mind.

You now can sleep late on Saturday mornings because your child can feed, clothe, and amuse herself. Your child probably has learned how to tell time, tie shoes, help with chores, count money, scramble eggs, care for animals, and make up games. Whatever limitations your child has, chances are you have been pleasantly surprised by some of her abilities and interests. Your child can reason effectively about increasingly complex problems. Your child has a definite personality, clear preferences, and a mind of her own. The "gimme-gimme" quality of the early years has been replaced by a self-control capable of saving for desired treasures, such as buying a catcher's mitt or ankle bracelet.

You have changed, too. Since the child is less given to throwing temper tantrums, so are you. You use reasoning more than discipline to shape behavior. Much of the weight of parental responsibility has lifted. You have more time for yourself and your work because you no longer have to be eternally vigilant about small fingers poking electrical sockets. You are back to going to the bathroom by yourself. The school system is responsible for your child during much of the day.

Just when you are beginning to think that being a parent can be fun and that children can be genuinely helpful, you find that things have not improved as much as you hoped. You may even feel that things have gotten decidedly worse. The child you have not slapped since he was five years old and swiped a candy bar has now become so sarcastic that you once more want to slap some sense into him. Come the second decade of parenthood, feelings escalate in intensity because old expectations and patterns prove to be inadequate. On bad days, you may feel that family life is disintegrating, you are an inept parent, and your child is regressing.

The strong emotions make sense if you consider what is happening. Children in the early primary grades are a joy because they are becoming so competent; it is a time when they are refining their understanding of the social world, developing self-control and self-regulation. You compare them to the babies they not long ago were, and you are thrilled by what they can do. But as children reach puberty and begin to look like adults, you no longer compare them to babies. You compare them to adults, and then find them lacking.

This is not only a period of rapid physical growth, but of dramatic change in the quality of their thinking. There is an increased capacity for hypothetico-deductive thinking, which means that these children are now capable of sarcasm, puns, irony, and putdowns. They exercise these newfound skills by criticizing and mocking. You wonder if you have not produced a truly obnoxious human being, for these accomplishments do not leave you always wanting to applaud their remarks. You are pleased that you reached midlife with some semblance of self-esteem, because interacting with your child can leave you feeling unstrung and stupid. Your behavior is constantly being judged by your child and you always seem to be found wanting. You decide that no child of yours is going to be so disrespectful, and take aim at the child with your own biting comments. The child is now angry at you for not behaving better— after all, you are the parent. Welcome to the second decade of parenthood!

The events of this period are little discussed. Both parents who have written about their own experiences and professionals who study family life have concentrated on describing and analyzing the first few years, because they are traditionally thought to be crucial in setting the stage for subsequent parent-child interactions. If there are strong feelings in the transition to parenthood, as there certainly are, the approach has been to discuss them in the hope of helping parents deal with them more effectively. The expectation is that some consideration of difficult times at this point will minimize their occurrence later.

When difficulties surface in the second decade of parenthood, they are frequently taken as proof that something has gone dreadfully wrong in the years gone by, rather than as an indication of the surfacing of new issues. To the extent that parents feel that something is wrong, they feel guilty. Feeling guilty, they are more likely to react to experiences than to analyze them. They react by wanting to control what they do not understand, just at a time when their children want to control their own destinies. This leads to many an explosive situation.

The purpose of this book is to explore as fully as possible the second decade of parenthood at this time in our society, in order to help parents act rather than just react. Parents need to realize that they have to be sensitive to new rhythms and learn new moves during these years. I believe that the second decade of parenthood, the letting-go period, calls for a very different approach from the first decade of parenthood, with its emphasis on attachment. The more you understand the dynamics shaping the behavior of children and parents during this time, the more you can facilitate positive exchanges. The emphasis throughout the book is not on specific problems but on common developmental changes. Minimally, the book should reassure parents hungry for information about their situation that many of their secret feelings and thoughts are typical of the experience. Optimally, understanding the dynamics of this period can lead to more effective ways of behaving. Hopefully, this book will be of use to professionals as well as to parents; for that reason, an extensive bibliography is provided.

There are many times when I refer to "you parents" as if all parents experience exactly the same thing. Keep in mind that this sort of phrasing is a literary device; I did not want to have to qualify every point with "on the one hand" then "on the other hand." Generalizations in this book are always meant to signify that something is not unusual, rather than to indicate that the statement is invariably true.

The first chapter communicates some information about why there is newfound interest in the growth and development of parents along with the growth and development of their children. The next two chapters describe what is presently known about adolescence and middlescence, because an understanding of the psychology of both the child and the parent is essential if their interactions with each other are to be deciphered. The next four chapters address specific themes that characterize this period, and the final chapter sketches out what you hope to have accomplished by the end of the second decade of parenthood.

A major help in clarifying my thinking while preparing this book was the remarks made by friends and associates when they heard that I was writing a book on the second decade of parenthood. They often told me that the book was needed,

then went on to say, "Of course, you're going to cover _____."
As soon as I could, after the conversation was over I wrote
down their comments for future reference. Besides these
notes, this book is based on an extensive review of the literature, personal experiences with two teenage daughters and
their friends, a series of formal interviews with parents in various family situations, and much eavesdropping. It took four
years of thinking about these matters to get to the point where
I thought that I could weave my impressions into a whole that
made sense out of all my data.

My intention was to write a book that would be general
enough to be of use to parents no matter what their particular
family configuration. I have tried, however, to provide many
examples as I flesh out key themes in order to make my points
come alive. The experts have admitted that the question of how
teenagers influence their parents has been largely unad-
dressed. My investigation of the issues convinces me that some
general themes characterize the second decade of parenthood.
For example, most parents are surprised to find how time con-
suming parenting at this period is; most parents are distressed
when their children dismiss them as dated, even if they once
did the same to their own parents; most parents are concerned
about saving their children from making mistakes, whereas
most children are more worried about whether their parents
will stand by them when they do make mistakes; most parents
are inclined to sermonize even though their children are tired
of monologues; most parents expect their children to feel
happy and contented even if they themselves have a long history of mood swings.

I think that the second decade of parenthood is a time of
powerful emotions. Strong bonds are always accompanied by
intense feelings. These feelings will include anger and resentment as well as pride and fondness, because close relationships
necessarily include the full spectrum of experience. To care

deeply means that you will care about everything the child does or does not do. The fact that our society prefers emotions sanitized and upbeat may leave parents thinking that their roller-coaster feelings at this time in their children's lives are abnormal. The truth is that this is likely to be a time when great emotional swings characterize the experience of both child and parent.

Let me end this introduction by recalling the comment of one statistics-minded father. He was lamenting how difficult it was to live with his son. He said, "My son is your *average* teenager. He is like all averages, what you get by combining extremes." I think that comment is insightful in entering into the subject matter of this book. In one sense, there is no such creature as the "average parent" or the "average teenager." To the extent that there are typical parent-child situations, they are a combination of many different extremes. We have to understand these diverse components in order to understand what is going on generally.

How To Enjoy
A GOOD LIFE
WITH YOUR TEENAGER

· 1 ·

THE GROWTH
AND DEVELOPMENT
OF PARENTS

Until recent times, no one talked in terms of the growth and development of parents. Parents *did* for children, and you expected them to do their best, but the parents' viewpoint was thought to be relatively inconsequential. Sure, you might have a perfunctory chapter on "Parents Have Feelings, Too" in a book on childrearing, but the impression usually conveyed was that those special feelings or concerns would last only as long as it took to read the twelve-page chapter. If you enrolled in a life-span development course during your college years, it probably took most of the semester to get to, much less through, adolescence. After that, it was only a short time before you were considering life during the retirement years. You did not pay much attention to the adult years, much less to parenthood as a key experience. People talked about *surviving* parenthood, especially when referring to life with teenagers, because it was conceptualized as a series of responsibilities to be fulfilled rather than as a developmental opportunity for the parents. Experts worried about the fate of children and not about the fate of adults, because grownups were thought to be all grown up and finished products.

Those tendencies have been contravened in the last two decades by three forces. First, the Women's Movement has spearheaded a major rethinking of parenthood; assumptions about what is involved in being a mother or father have been reexamined. Second, the traditional focus on the effects of parents on their children has been supplanted, to some extent, by a recognition that children are important determiners of their parents' behavior. Third, our aging population is critical of society's preoccupation with the experience of youth and is calling for comparable intensive study of adult development across the life cycle; this means paying attention to parenthood as a key experience during the adult years. In order to set the stage for why an analysis of the second decade of parenthood is important, this chapter will address each of these trends in turn.

The Women's Movement has had a tremendous effect on our thinking about parenthood. The two individuals most associated with the midcentury revival of the Women's Movement soundly criticized the traditional role of mother in Western society. Simone de Beauvoir noted that motherhood as woman's ultimate fulfillment was nothing more than an advertising slogan: "There is an extravagant fraudulence in the easy reconciliation made between the common attitude of contempt for women and the respect shown for mothers."[1] In *The Second Sex*, which contained the first widely read feminist analysis of woman as mother, she argued for honest, realistic perceptions of the role. More than a decade later, Betty Friedan thought it was sick of mothers to live vicariously through their children; it was "a disease in the shape of a progressively weaker core of human self that is being handed down to their sons and daughters at a time when the dehumanizing aspects of modern mass culture make it necessary for men and women to have a strong core of self."[2] She believed that if women are allowed to develop themselves, they will, in turn, do a better job of overseeing the development of their children.

These criticisms have been echoed and further developed by many writers in the last twenty plus years. Betty Rollin wrote that motherhood was in trouble—"Who needs it?"[3] Jane Lazarre described "the mother knot"[4] of thwarted expectations. Adrienne Rich deprecated motherhood as experience and institution.[5] Shirley Radl lamented the enormity of the contradictions that she felt as a mother: "How was it possible for me to genuinely love my children and yet not like—often to the point of resentment—nearly everything associated with the role of motherhood?"[6] Rochelle Paul Wortis noted that changes in the maternal role might have positive consequences for changing the kind of children we raise.[7] Vivian Gornick said, "Woman-the-mother is the golden ideal, the convenient repository for man's most unexamined, sentimentalized, suffocating, ahuman notions about his own composite being."[8] There was general consensus that the poetic accolades showered on motherhood did not offset the difficulties experienced by individuals in that role, and that something must be done to make the experience more positive for women.

It was thought that motherhood would be more likely to be a positive experience for women if the discrepancy between expectations and reality was better understood. For example, women may expect the experience to leave them feeling madonna patient and earth-mother generous, when being responsible for a child can actually be an isolating and exhausting experience. Another discrepancy considered to be in need of investigation was the one between the infant's *absolute* need for a caregiver and the caregiver's *relative* need to play that role. When women become mothers, they continue to function as wives, daughters, sisters, workers, and friends, so the role of caregiver has to be one negotiated in relationship to other roles. It cannot exist removed from other societal connections. A large portion of the feminist debate focused on how you could meet the needs of others *and* meet your own needs, too.

There was no doubt that a person who did not attend to her own needs would have little to give others, but just how you managed to be self-enhancing while doing for others was less clear.

Not only was the traditional role of mother criticized for burdening women with total responsibility for childrearing, but this rethinking encouraged extensive new consideration of the participation of the father in family life. There were those who thought the cure of choice for the overbearing mother was the restoration of the absent father to the family circle. Children need to interact with both parents in order to blossom. Even those men not ideologically committed to feminism were beginning to see the wisdom of being involved with their children in their early years in order to make it more likely that their children would stay involved with them when they reached adulthood.

The 1970s were characterized by a plethora of books, aimed at both the professional and lay markets, on the father-child relationship. Whole issues of journals were devoted to fatherhood and men's roles in the family. They covered topics as varied as "The Biological Bases of the Paternal Responses," "Men's Entrance to Parenthood," "Divorced Fathers," "The Special Role of Stepfather," and "Fathers and the Postparental Transition." By 1981, Michael Lamb was writing, "Having demonstrated *that* fathers affect child development, we now need to determine *how* and *how much*."[9] The search was on to discover how fathers can be a positive force and also profit from their role in families.

One way that fathers were thought to profit from parenthood was in learning more about themselves. In his diary account of his relationship with his six-month-old son, David Steinberg describes how he was changed by the experience:

> Being with Dylan gives me a chance to express my intuitive, feminine, yin-self. As a man, it's easy to

always be in situations that call for aggressive, rational, manipulative perspectives and skills. With Dylan I move out of that more completely than I ever have before. As a result I feel myself growing in all kinds of new ways. The clear importance of these new skills in caring for Dylan helps me respect and value them as they develop.[10]

This father is developing a new repertoire of behaviors and, simultaneously, a respect for the care ethic.

This massive rethinking of what it means to be a mother or father took place against the backdrop of an increasingly contraceptive society. Pregnancy was no longer the price you paid for having a sex life; it was now possible to decide whether you wanted to have any children, when and how many you would have. This was thought to be an encouraging development; many believed that couples who wait to have children would probably be more mature in handling the experience of parenthood. Having a choice means individuals presumably have weighed the pros and cons, and concluded that the values of having children outweigh any disadvantages. This deliberative process suggests that the adult expects the role to be self-enhancing. Parents expect that children will expand them—tapping new dimensions of their personality—and provide stimulation, novelty, and amusement.

With all the ZPG (zero population growth) talk about "None is fun," those who now made the decision to become a parent had higher expectations that this experience, freely chosen, would generate personal development: "It gives us an opportunity to refine and express who we are, to learn what we can be, to become someone different. . . . Parenthood is one of the major growth-promoting experiences of adulthood."[11] Today's parents, it was thought, need not just react to the forces of nature, but would be able to shape their destiny. If you could decide when to have a baby, you should be able to influence the quality of the years to come. Anyway that was the hope.

The very fact that this book focuses on "parenthood"—an egalitarian term—is an indication of a major shift, for too often "motherhood" and "fatherhood" have been conceptualized in terms of sexual stereotypes. Traditionally, mothers and fathers have been expected to act differently—experiencing different feelings, responsibilities, and expectations—and that was what the Women's Movement opposed. For example, Louise Bates Ames has described the roles of father and mother thus: "Father's primary goal may be to support his family; mother's may be not only to keep everybody fed, clothed, and looked after but, hopefully, to keep everybody happy."[12] But that view is destructive to women because it expects the impossible—keeping everybody happy—and reinforces the notion that the father should spend his days away from the family as breadwinner. This functional view separates considerations of nurturance and compassion from those of power and strength. By contrast, being a parent presupposes a different philosophical stance. It means a new balance, not a diminution of virtues, but "a balance within each sex rather than a balance between them."[13] Such balanced parenting "would leave people of both genders with the positive capacities each has, but without the destructive extremes these currently tend toward."[14]

"Parenting" does not conjure up romantic images of complete self-sacrifice or devotion. It does imply a commitment to meet the needs of the next generation, kindliness, protectiveness, continuity of care, and respect for the dignity of children. The word suggests some sort of equal and/or reciprocal relationship between the mother and the father in their dealings with their children. Once you think of parenting, rather than mothering or fathering, you are free to think about how to divide the task of parenting in new ways that might develop the growth potential of all concerned.

To parent implies an investment in the next generation. It is an oppportunity to resolve some of the unfinished business of your own childhood, as well as to shape the attitudes and values of those to come. Being a parent does not mean "giving up" but "taking on," for it brings new emotions, responsibilities, and possibilities. As Margaret Mead once said, "I grasp the meaning of puckered eyebrows, a tensed hand, or a light flick of the tongue. The known and loved particular child makes it possible for one to understand better and care more about all children." [15]

One incentive for eschewing a functional division of labor in the home, in favor of shared parenting, is that children are more likely to learn how to be balanced themselves from parents who each combine both instrumental and expressive qualities. The old view of woman as heart of the family and man as head of the family assumed that the child would learn how to feel and to think by observing her caring and his reasoning. But emphasis on two separate domains makes it more difficult rather than easier to imagine combining both aspects in one person. It is in observing how individuals balance matters of the heart with reason and matters of the mind with caring that children learn to do the same. All families can use at least two adult heads and two adult hearts!

Elizabeth Janeway wrote about how all adults can profit from parenting:

> One learns a good deal about time—that it passes and yet remains solid as experience. One learns that life changes even if one sits still, when it's wise to sit still, and when it isn't. Most of all, one learns other people and one's own limits in terms of relationships with them. All this is important learning, but let us once again refrain from supposing that it is learned only by women and valuable only to them.

It is the kind of knowledge that is learned on the way to maturity no matter how the path winds.[16]

In this view, the parent teaches, and learns, in turn, many valuable lessons.

This new view of parenting ran counter to the hackneyed praise of mothers embroidered on pillows—"M" is for the many things she did for me—but also searched for evidence that parenting could be a positive experience for the adults. It came to mean ideally answering your children's inevitable question, "Did you ever wish you never had us?" by saying what Letty Cottin Pogrebin did: "Sometimes my life is a little too full because I have you children, but, for me, it would be much too empty if I didn't."[17] This sentiment is very different from the cloying messages found on most Mother's Day cards, and communicates both some normal tensions and the promise of a rich experience.

No consideration of how the Women's Movement has affected our rethinking of parenthood can ignore the extent to which feminists have emphasized consciousness raising, which has led to a renewed appreciation for the importance of reflecting on everyday experiences and relationships. Consciousness raising is commonsense expression of concepts; it means viewing ordinary thoughts and feelings as worthy of serious analysis. Since the critical reconstitution of the meaning of women's experiences as they live through them is central to feminist theory and feminist methods, the day-to-day impressions of women, in the role considered to be the most fulfilling of all, assume special importance.

Until recent times, the perceptions of women were not deemed worthy of intense scrutiny. The childcare experts, largely male, regularly discounted the mother's viewpoint in favor of the prevailing theory of childrearing. Her worries about her children were often dismissed as neurotic; her concerns about herself were regarded as unduly narcissistic. But if women are to thrive in the role of parent, then systematic study of their experience as captured in diaries and coffee klatch discussions is important. In reflecting on the activities of daily living, knotted expectations are unraveled. Tortured feelings are not to be guiltily squelched, but decoded for fresh insights about relationships. If you do not feel moo-cow contentment as a mother, then the problem may be in the popular conceptualization of the role, not in you as an individual. Coffee mugs that read, "God couldn't be everywhere, so He invented mothers," may be more of a clue to expectations than an academic treatise on roles.

It is not just in criticizing the existing order or in demanding personally satisfying interpersonal relationships that the Women's Movement has led the way in rethinking parenthood. Feminists have repeatedly maintained that the lived experience is valuable and can serve as the springboard to innovation, thereby setting the stage for the analysis of commonplace thoughts and feelings in this book. When you take seriously the fact that many parents "jokingly" speak of their children becoming teenagers in a way that conjures up images of werewolf transformations, you appreciate the need to understand better what is going on during this period.

While proponents of the Women's Movement were becoming increasingly concerned in the 1970s about whether families encouraged the growth of all members, a revolution of sorts was taking place in the social sciences. The traditional assumption that parents influence their children—family relations are unidirectional—was put into question. (Many would question the use of the word "parents" here, for most often children were viewed as the product of the mother's behavior.) Professionals became concerned with the extent to which children influence their parents. Previously such effects, when acknowledged, were downplayed.

Why did the paradigm of causality shift at this point? Certainly social scientists were becoming increasingly aware of how complex behavior is. They became skeptical of the validity of any unidirectional view and more oriented to reciprocal relationships among family members. One reason this new perspective may have emerged when it did was because by 1970 the teenage population of the United States was 20 million. Their dress, music, and values seemed to take over the rest of society; many adults no longer felt that they had much influence over their children. This sense that adults were on the receiving end, not in the driver's seat, may have seemed particularly pronounced because only unidirectional change was expected. Anything else had a jolting effect.

There can be no doubt, however, that the 1970s represented a move away from a simplistic model of causality to an awareness of the effects of children on parents. One of the first areas to be extensively analyzed was infant crying as an elicitor of parental behavior; not coincidentally, this was an area much discussed in diary accounts of parenting. Both professionals and the public were coming to appreciate that adults begin parenting shaped by their child's cry:

> Young parents are at the mercy of a cry, and further, can't escape the compelling quality of the infant's facial expression and the helpless, thrashing movements once the cry has brought them within visual range. Parents with a firstborn seem not only overwhelmed with their new responsibilities but also somewhat helpless and confused. In many respects, they appear to be much less powerful than the infant, whose behaviors are remarkably well organized to produce a given result. [18]

Many parents would be quick to add that they have also gone through their children's subsequent years waiting for the positive reinforcement of a smile, hug or compliment, and that their children's behavior always seems remarkably well organized to produce a given result.

Newborns are now no longer viewed as clean slates on which one can write anything, but as capable of immediately acting on their environments. They are recognized as competent organisms who exhibit decided preferences. Whether they are adaptable and consolable affects their caregivers; the degree to which a child's behavior is clear and predictable influences parent-child interaction with each other, but also the timing of the behavior—what each does *in response* to the behavior of the other—that shapes consequent exchange. The responsivity of one is thought to be a powerful stimulus to the other. Contingent positive responses, of course, have one effect, while contingent negative responses have another.

All parents are no longer thought to be presented with comparable tasks; children vary in their conformability. It is much more difficult for parents to handle a child who tends to be fussy, demanding, and unsmiling than one who laughs frequently, listens attentively, and seems easy to please. Parents like a child who makes them look effective; they respond well when the child seems to be bringing out their best.

By definition, parent-child relations have a chicken-or-egg quality about them. The behavior of the parent may influence the child, but the child's resultant action then shapes the reaction of the parent, and another sequence of behavior is under way. There is mutual regulation, for the child serves as a stimulus to the parent by eliciting, motivating, rewarding, and punishing parental action, and vice versa. As Barclay Martin reminds us, "Almost any association of a given type of parent behavior with a given type of child behavior can be interpreted in terms of the parent influencing the child or the child influencing the parent. . . ."[19] Parents may alter their child, but the changes that they have wrought in the child regularly affect them in turn. Through the feedback children receive, they become active shapers of their own development. All who write in this area would seem willing to agree with the quip of Peter de Vries, "The value of marriage is not that adults produce children, but that children produce adults."[20]

Researchers have just begun to acknowledge fully the reciprocal effects of children on parents, and the process of how parent and child socialize each other for a relationship that will be of primary importance throughout their lives. There seems to be widespread agreement that children are determiners of their parents' behavior, but very few examples of this mutual regulation have been provided regarding the second decade of parenthood. Yet that is a time when children may be less likely to give their parents a contingent positive response, perhaps making parents less likely to do the same for their children. Of what consequence is this? It has been said that children "are most lovable when they are most egocentric and most disruptive and threatening to family morale in adolescence when they have become most competent and prosocial."[21] From a systems perspective, why is this the case? Is it because the child's neediness makes parents feel needed, while independence causes them to feel set aside?

None of the trends addressed in this chapter exists in separation from the others. The insistence in the Women's Movement that parenthood should be a growth-enhancing experience and the acknowledgment of the reciprocal effects of children on parents have in common the notion that having children changes you. Both of these trends, in turn, were taking shape in a period when efforts at specifying the stages and themes of adult development were capturing the interest of many. Researchers with an orientation to life-span development became concerned about parenthood as a key role in adult development. David Gutmann argues, for example, that "parenthood constitutes the pivotal stage of the human life cycle, organizing the form and content of the stages which lead up to it as well as those that succeed it."[22]

Erik Erikson's eight life stages was the only widely known model concerned about adult development until the 1970s.[23] The adult years were largely ignored because issues of growth and development tended to be linked to periods of somatic change. Maturity was equated with physical maturity, the end of puberty. The adult years were thought to be a time of steadiness, until the body started to weaken and deteriorate. Developmentalists were writing about the "Terrible Twos," but no one considered it suitable to comment on the "Angst-Filled Forty-Twos." Psychologically, the person who reached the adult years relatively free of neurotic fixations, was expected to live relatively happily ever after, not unlike the way the prince and princess did in all those fairy tales. The temperament and coping skills formed during childhood would inform behavior during the adult years. Erikson's work was the major exception to this viewpoint, though even his model still devoted five life stages to detailing the developmental tasks of childhood and adolescence, and only three to the long adult years. And he apparently first thought these developmental stages should read downward, not upward.[24]

In Erikson's schema, "Generativity vs. Self-Absorption" is the central theme of maturity. For him, generativity leads to a gradual expansion of ego interests in order to avoid individual stagnation. Erikson argues that each developmental task has its time of special ascendancy, and that "intimacy," the task of young adulthood, is followed by an investment in "generativity." In this view, becoming fully mature implies moving away from being self-centered to being willing to establish and guide others. New affiliations are made. Care and commitment to obligations become the earmarks of an ethic that informs the lives of mature adults; they are willing to nurture others. Those who refuse to take up this challenge become increasingly self-absorbed and develop constricted personalities. Although you do not have to become a parent in order to go beyond self-interest, raising a child is a highly personal way of showing concern for others—and of learning concern for others.

By the end of the 1960s, writing about adult development increased noticeably. Erikson's stages were no longer all that was generally known about the course of the life cycle. A conviction was growing that development is a lifelong process, and attention was being drawn to the second half of the life span. So absorbed were developmentalists in adulthood that they started dividing those years into different periods—young adulthood, middle adulthood, young olds, old olds. In the seventies, Roger Gould wrote about the phases of adult life,[25] Daniel Levinson and his associates sketched out seasons of a man's life,[26] George Vaillant reflected on men's adaptation to life,[27] and Gail Sheehy detailed the predictable crises of adult life.[28]

New phrases became part of public consciousness; people talked about the "Trying Twenties," "BOOM" (becoming one's own man), and the "Age 40 Crucible." Gail Sheehy's article on "Catch-30" in *New York* magazine broke all records for reader response; hundreds wrote in saying, "You're writing about me."[29] The tremendous need adults have to understand themselves better became apparent.

Parenthood, as such, is relatively little discussed in the work of Levinson, Vaillant, and Sheehy; their emphasis is on work commitment and career progression. The emergence of nurturance is discussed principally in terms of becoming a mentor to junior colleagues at work. This is probably the case because the first two focused exclusively on the experience of men, and Sheehy's study was derivative, based largely on Levinson's work. Gould, who studied both women and men, did note a general midlife change connected with parenting: "There is a turning away from an active social life outside the family to a focus on their own children and a reconsideration of their parents' mistakes with them while they are considering their mistakes with their own children."[30] This suggests a time of reflection.

No brief overview can adequately describe the extent of current interest in adult development. Some models detail normative life crises (e.g., the work of Gould, Levinson, Vaillant, Sheehy), but other models do not hold that adult development is paced by crises, but by a sense of "average expectable life cycle."[31] Chronological age, in this view, is not necessarily a meaningful marker because the timing of major life events (e.g., marriage, birth of first child, last child leaving home) varies from individual to individual. It is important to note that many of the life events considered to be major involve expanding family size then letting go of children. Allowing for the range of opinion that characterizes the field of human development, parenthood does emerge as a key role in adult development, even if it has not always been center stage in all discussions of the adult years.

In the last two decades, parenthood has been increasingly seen as a role providing a framework for viewing continuity and change over the entire life cycle. For example, Therese Benedek believes that ". . . parenthood implies continuous adaptation to physiologic and psychologic changes within the self of the parent parallel to, and in transaction with, changes in the child and to his expanding world."[32] Like Erik Erikson before him, Robert White considers the expansion of caring to be a feature of the adult years: "Becoming a parent often produces a fairly sudden enlargement of one's cognitive map."[33] Children draw you into being concerned about the world at large—pediatric services, museum offerings, school programs, summer jobs for teenagers, highway safety, cultural enrichment, community services, etc. In caring for the child, you begin to care more for all the people, rules, and institutions that touch the child.

There is mounting evidence that becoming a parent is a major source of change. It forces individuals to learn new skills and to develop further those already learned. As one woman said, "It's necessary that you change when you have children and you need to change really rapidly sometimes. . . . I've changed and I think I'm a better person now."[34] However, the changes that apply to the second decade of parenthood have never been described in much detail. Most of what has been written about that period is problem oriented; difficulties are the focus, not development.

This packed discussion of three distinct, but connected, trends was meant to set the stage for the remainder of this book. Not only has the general subject been put into a context, but the nature of my own intellectual history has also been articulated. My thinking has been shaped by each one of these movements, and I make some basic assumptions as a result: What it means to be a mother or father is in the process of being rethought. Traditional views of parenting often ignore the lived experience of individuals in these roles; everyday experiences are worthy of study. Parenthood is a key role in adult development; being a parent changes you. Children affect parents in complicated ways, but relatively little is known about how the behavior of the parent may influence the teenager and how the child's resultant action then shapes the reaction of the parent. A conviction is growing that one has to consider the growth and development of parents if one is truly determined to facilitate the growth and development of their children. A developmental approach to the subject matter, as opposed to focusing only on problems, permits better understanding of the total experience.

With these assumptions in mind, let us examine both adolescents and their parents at closer range. It is important to remember that we set off to understand the experience of each generation with a very different set of assumptions than would have been the case not long ago. This means a fresh perspective is open to us.

· 2 ·

DREAMERS

Adolescence is a transition period from dependent childhood to self-sufficient adulthood. As such, teenagers (and we refer to those ages ten, eleven, and twelve as pre-teens because they are already beginning to experience the changing identity associated with the teen years) spend their days suspended between two better defined poles. They are no longer unformed children clinging to their parents, but they still depend on their parents for emotional and material support. These girl-women and boy-men dangle:

> They are not adults capable of carrying the adult responsibilities we confer upon them. And they are not children whose subservience to adults can be taken for granted. We expect them to be grown up in all those domains where we cannot or do not want to maintain control. But in other domains, such as attending school, we expect our teenagers to behave like obedient children.[1]

This suggests that there is often disagreement between the generations concerning those areas where responsibility is expected and some obedience is required, and that control is an important issue.

Parents may welcome some changes—those clearly indicating that the child is becoming more responsible—but may have great difficulty with the change process as such. Change may sometimes look like caprice, fitfulness, discontinuity, divergence, uncertainty, irresoluteness, and irascibility. All those components are normally associated with the change process, but they are not necessarily regarded as positive. Comfortable, familiar ways of relating no longer seem to work; the known child may seem like a stranger.

Teenagers need a protected time within which to construct a personal identity—one when a bogus maturity is not thrust upon them. But many of their actions do not trigger protectiveness in their parents the way silky skin and cherub curves once did. Many of their behaviors seem far removed from positive development; the child shouts for self-determination but regularly seems incapable of handling modest responsibilities. The adults sometimes feel like washing their hands of this child who seems impossible to figure out and who leaves them feeling drained and helpless. It is also sometimes difficult to distinguish between being the child's protector and acting like a warden.

What are teenagers like? Ask most parents that question and they will mention stereotyped behaviors. Teenagers are constantly on the phone talking with friends. When not on the phone, they are either out with these friends cruising shopping malls, going to the movies and doing Lord knows what else, or hibernating in their poster-filled, clothes-strewn rooms listening to blaring rock music.

Teenagers are moody, opinionated creatures full of passionate loves and hates. They *love* clothes, cars, and the gorgeous body that has the locker next to them. They *hate* people who are phonies, going places with their parents, and being told what to do. They gleefully point out to you the error of your ways, but cannot tolerate any criticisms—no matter how justified—of them. They want their uniqueness to be appreciated, but wear jeans and shirts stamped out of the same mold.

They want to be taken seriously, but feel essentially misunderstood. They are fired up by outside interests, but have little energy for chores at home. They complain about leading a boring life, but their complaints are themselves tedious. They question the religious beliefs of their parents, but believe in developing their own codes of ethics. They are pure id, but censorious; they are disapproving, but enjoy being gross. They are "holier than thou," but do not want to listen to their parents' sermons. They cannot bear friends who cannot keep a secret, but spend hours gossiping. They embrace the future, but despair over finishing the current semester of school. They are dreamers in search of a vision.

It is important to note from the onset that teenagers are much more complicated and dissimilar than these characterizations suggest, but these descriptions hold in a surface way because the underlying developmental tasks of this period affect all with some regularity. These developmental tasks can be summarized thus:

> If the adolescent is to become truly adult, not just physically mature, he must, in the few short years between childhood and nominal adulthood, gradually achieve independence from his family; adjust to his sexual maturation; establish cooperative and workable relationships with his peers, without being dominated by them; and decide on and prepare for a meaningful vocation. In the process, he must develop a philosophy of life, that is, a set of guiding moral beliefs and standards which can lend

some order and consistency to the many decisions he will have to make and the actions he will have to take in a diverse, changing, sometimes chaotic world. And he must develop a sense of his own identity. Before the adolescent can safely abandon the security of childhood dependence on others, he must have some idea of who he is, where he is going, and what the possibilities are of getting there.[2]

And it is not just each "he" who asks, "Who am I?" This agenda applies equally to girls in our society. Any observed sex differences in identity development can be interpreted as a function of cultural influences rather than as the unfolding of different developmental capabilities.

The list of what needs to be accomplished during these years is long. Though the developmental tasks of childhood—learning to trust, toilet training, language comprehension, impulse control, etc.—are many, they are not as far-reaching as those of adolescence. Not only are specific aspects of the adolescent maturing (e.g., maturation of the physique, sexuality, and intellectual skills), but the individual's relationship to the world at large is also preparing for a quantum leap. All the single physiologic and psychologic accomplishments now have to be woven together into a seamless identity ready for social, occupational, and interpersonal responsibilities.

No wonder teenagers are constantly in touch with their friends; you need to gossip in order to feel in touch with things, and you need to exchange thoughts and feelings in order to get a hold of them. No wonder teenagers have great needs for privacy; in listening for your own voice, you can hope to hear it. No wonder teenagers argue with their parents; it is in articulating your own ideas and values that they can begin to seem real. No wonder teenagers seem to be chameleons; by trying on different attitudes and seeing how various situations shape you, you can eventually find that part of you that is solid and unchangeable. No wonder teenagers want to be seen as more up-to-date than their staid parents, but regard parents who do not act their age as irresponsible; it is only possible to move on with confidence if the markers indicating where you have been are in place.

No wonder teenagers are both indulgent and ascetic; it is in oscillating between being self-centered and being self-sacrificing that the self can be created. No wonder teenagers love the unusual; in being trendy, they hope to convince themselves that they can be pacesetters, and by championing the underdog they strive to make the whole world more receptive to those who do not seem to fit in easily (including themselves). No wonder teenagers want to decorate their bodies; in staring at the mirror, you hope to see yourself as others see you. No wonder teenagers get carried away with outside enthusiasms and then come to a sluggish halt when they return home; by extending yourself, you learn new things, but there has to be a nest to which you return. And teenagers may think a nest is properly made up of strewn clothes, empty soda cans, crumpled papers, psychedelic posters, and music that speaks to the unconscious!

The developmental tasks of adolescence may be more far-reaching than those of childhood, but adults do not necessarily link the everyday behavior that they see with development. Some of it looks like regression to them. The negativism, fidgetiness, impulsivity, and "I want what I want when I want it" of the toddler, which was greatly modified during the early school years, now seems to resurface. Psychoanalysts would agree with the parent who sees regression, for they describe adolescence as having the distinction of being the only period of life where regression is part of the maturational process. Adolescence has been pictured as a new edition of the infantile period prompted by the pressure of instincts. The onrush of new impulses confronts a still underdeveloped ego, and the result is a period of wild seesawing between blind submission and defiant rebellion, between egotism and self-sacrifice, between instinctual indulgence and lofty idealism, between lighthearted optimism and the blackest pessimism.

Some behaviors may look infantile, but this is a recapitulation with a big difference: "The regressive processes of adolescence permit the remodeling of defective or incomplete earlier developments."[3] What may look on the surface like the knee-jerk negativism of the toddler period is an obstinacy that has as its purpose bringing into focus the child's unique point of view. Instinctual processes are translated into intellectual terms, so they may be mastered on a different psychic level. For example, powerful longings may be transformed into lengthy arguments about the human race's inability to be monogamous over a lifetime.

Those moments when children seem to be pure id, the pleasure principle incarnate, they seem so far removed from becoming mature that it is difficult to recognize their behavior as evidence of growth of any kind. But an underlying purposefulness is there. Unless you recognize that, you will be tempted to concentrate on extinguishing the selfish, indulgent, exhibitionistic, lazy tendencies. You want the child to shape up and act adult, but she or he is not yet at that point. The habits of cleanliness acquired by the age of nine may have been displaced by a certain amount of dirt and disorder, and you are afraid that the mess will escalate if you do not lay down the law. Chances are that you are exaggerating the chaos because any apparent regression gets interpreted as progress stopped forever. That makes parents nervous. They imagine that the behavior of today will continue, if unchecked, forever and ever and ever. Parents are quick to overgeneralize; one act is an indication of a pattern. Their children try out different behaviors in order to see which pattern, if any, will fit them.

If you are able to put the child's behavior into a context, then you are able to recognize that individual instances of seemingly negative behavior are part of a larger whole. The developmental tasks of this period are difficult to see; that is one reason parent-child relations are often strained at this time. When you watch young children move from having lousy aim with a spoon to getting food neatly into their mouths, you know that this is a major accomplishment. Alas, the tasks of adolescence are not as neat and delimited as keeping your pants dry, learning how to write your name, or mastering the jump shot. To forge a sense of identity—the central task of adolescence—involves the messy business of arguing, rebelling, posturing, preening, and doing one's own thing. These behaviors can escape a negative label only if they are put into a context.

What is the context into which behavior should be put? Individual instances of behavior should be considered as reflections of complicated development in progress. Pick up a book on adolescent life experiences and you will see the work in progress discussed at length: the attainment of physical maturity, resolution of concerns about body image, the emergence of sexuality, the forging of self-esteem, and the development of gender-role adequacy, identity, values, vocational interests, satisfactory peer relations, and new family relations. The teenager's behavior is neither as shallow nor as purposeless as it sometimes seems to be; it is shaped by many grave concerns. But the trying on of behaviors looks messy if it is not understood as steps on the way to important outcomes.

The most observable differences during this time involve physical maturation. Breasts bud. Voices deepen. Hips broaden. Shoulders widen. Facial, underarm, and pubic hair appear. Children gain height, stop looking up to their parents, and start looking down on them. Hormones fluctuate and so do moods. The onset of menstruation and the appearance of nocturnal emissions are proof positive, if any was needed, that one door has been closed and another one has been opened.

These transformations leave children worrying about their attractiveness more than ever before; acne does nothing to help the situation. This can be a particularly difficult time for those who deviate from the norm; early-maturing girls and late-maturing boys tend to feel extremely self-conscious. Rapid growth can leave individuals feeling grotesque, lumpy, dislocated, and out of control; delayed growth can leave individuals obsessed about whether they are normal.

Not only are adolescents worried about whether they are physically attractive, but they are also concerned to have their sexual identity affirmed. They want to be found womanly or manly—to be popular. They are working out how they are going to respond to various social conventions, not the least of which is how they are going to handle themselves sexually. As developmentalists remind us, "Intrapsychic and interpersonal sexual scripts and their articulation with other aspects of personality become for most individuals one of the most enduring and influential of the outcomes of adolescence."[4] "Falling in love" and "going steady" are important for certifying gender-role adequacy as much as they serve sexual interests. Wearing someone's school ring is some assurance that you will be able to find a lifelong partner. It is a confusing time. Society does a good job of making adolescents fear both sexual experience and sexual inexperience, and this is only one reflection of more global conflict. Adolescents feel pushed and pulled, heeded and ignored, strange and ordinary—all at the same time.

These physical changes power the complicated process of individuation now under way. If you have literally grown up, shouldn't you be more your own person? Whereas becoming attached to parents and making their beliefs yours promotes the development of the young child, becoming differentiated from parents and learning to articulate your own values promotes the development of the adolescent. To do this involves some struggle, but it is a mistake to describe this contrariness as mean and hateful.

Opposition is important in that it makes clear to all concerned that one is autonomous. As Jerome Kagan reminds us, rebellion "does not primarily serve hostility, but rather is a product of the more pressing need to persuade the self that its configuration of wishes, values and behaviors derives from a personally constructed philosophy."[5] It is an important part of being taken seriously and taking yourself seriously.

Adolescents continue to need their parents' approval, even if they shrug their shoulders and seem to discount it when it is presented. The cry, "My parents don't understand me," testifies to the continuing need for parental approval, for you do not feel strongly about being misunderstood unless being found intelligible matters to you. Adolescents want to be found inscrutable because that signifies their separateness, but they also seek reassurance that their parents are still there, caring and approving. That sense of being misunderstood by one's parents serves some purpose if it is not extreme; it means that the teenager is unique and special in some way. Can you truly come into your own if those important to you see you as unchanged, without any mystery? The child may be annoyed when her parents do not seem to understand her, but she is also pleased that they are forced to devote so much time to figuring her out. The parents, however, may feel perplexed since they never expected to have to function as lay psychoanalysts. They long for the strange to be replaced by the familiar. In their minds, "family" and "familiar" go hand in hand.

Friendships with peers blossom at this time, partly because they provide the approval for the teenager's new look which parents may find difficult to give. Adolescents must be capable of intimacy among equals if they are ever to be ready to establish their own families one day. Confidences that might raise parents' eyebrows can be discussed comfortably with friends going through similar experiences. For example, as teenagers struggle with figuring out why they should achieve in school— "Who am I doing this for anyway?"—they cannot reasonably talk this over with parents who may become apoplectic at their merely raising the question. Yet if young people do not ask the question, they will put off making a commitment to their own agenda. How can you affirm the direction you are taking without knowing you had a choice? The only real truths are those that one builds freely oneself; ready-made answers do not satisfy.

Adolescents need those hundreds of hours of conversation to get clear about all those issues, which, if expressed to parents, might lead the adults to fret—or worse yet, to make fun of them. Teenagers want to be taken seriously, and they want to be in the company of people who take them seriously. It is reassuring to have friends who can answer you helpfully the many times you ask, "Do you think I did the right thing?" Asked the same question, parents are inclined to give what they take to be the correct answer, whereas friends are more likely to invite the questioner to think out loud.

The torturous process of figuring out who you are—some realistic balance of talents, limitations, and possibilities—is made possible only by cognitive advances that occur at this time. Whereas younger children are concrete in their thinking (e.g., they take proverbs very literally; they think "a rolling stone gathers no moss" applies only to rocks), the development of formal operational reasoning allows adolescents "to place a given problem in a context of possibilities, of which the observable reality is but a single class."[6] Not only is the teenager able to think hypothetically about various possibilities, but he can also envision the impossible. Perfection and the ideal can be imagined.

Problems can be defined, similarities noticed, and planning

starts to become an important cognitive strategy. Alas, worrying may be the price adolescents pay for becoming capable of anticipating the future. Now that they can imagine so much, they have more to worry about—their worth, what their life's work will be, whether they should go to college, and, if so, which one. The adolescent is capable of metacognition, and can now think about thoughts; this change makes introspection fully possible. For the first time, the child is equipped to puzzle about the meaning of life. This ability coupled with the growing need to commune with something larger than themselves leads teenagers to be open to idealistic commitments, gangs, and causes. They may decide to join a group that represents appealing ideals in the hope of being able to join forces with like-minded visionaries in order to make a mark on the world.

Argumentativeness is a function, in part, of new powers; now that teenagers can debate effectively, they want to exercise their skills. By seesawing back and forth between positions, they determine their own center of gravity. Formal operational thinking also means that the adolescent can use puns, parody, metaphors, sarcasm, irony, and satire with zest. Poetry—with its shaded meanings, haunting symbols, and rich feeling tones—may become for the first time a pleasure to read and write. Wordplays become staples of conversation. The child to whom so much once had to be explained now has to help parents understand the point of a particularly convoluted joke.

Ego development is facilitated by these cognitive advances. Obviously new skills, when admired, build confidence. These skills also enable teenagers to develop a sense of perspective about themselves as they internalize self-evaluated standards. If one can reflect on experiences over time, being called "stupid" or "ugly" has less effect; you can analyze that accusation in light of all the considerable evidence to the contrary.

Though a sense of perspective is now possible, teenagers still have only limited life experience. They can reflect on what happens to them, but they are also vulnerable to jumping to the wrong conclusions. One or two losses, particularly if they involve issues of attractiveness or popularity, can leave teenagers convinced that they are doomed to repeat these failures again and again. This partially explains why depression is such a problem for some teenagers. They do not have much experience with putting themselves back together after a disappointment, so they may be convinced that the despondency of the present will encase them forevermore.

Parents respond to these various developments with many emotions. The physical changes can be a source of pleasure— "You look the way I always wanted to look; if I couldn't be that pretty (or handsome or tall or petite or athletic), I'm glad someone in my family got to look that way"—but often they are a source of discomfort. The child is physically uncoordinated or chubby, and you are reminded that you have (or had) that problem, too. The parent looks at the curves and makeup, and worries that the daughter is turning into a tarty Lolita; the son's tight jeans may convey a horniness that is equally disconcerting. The child who once gave off innocent, helpless vibrations that made you feel nurturing now looks like the person who became your sexual partner. That is unnerving; it is also a reason for distancing yourself from the child. The child, of course, is becoming fully aware of her or his sexuality, and may feel drawn to the attractiveness of the parent of the other sex; the old goodnight caresses become awkward and another barrier goes up between the generations. Increased physical distance can lead to a sense of psychological distance; the parents feel removed from the child and the child feels removed from the parents.

The thirteen-year-old "falls in love" three times in one semester, and the parent starts worrying about promiscuity. The sixteen-year-old "goes steady," and the parent sermonizes on not getting too serious ("You should play the field"), only to be told: "In your day, going out with different people meant one thing; now it means you're indiscriminate. I don't want a bad reputation." You wonder what she and he are talking about in their five times daily phone calls. You imagine declarations of love, sighs, passionate promises, and overhear some serious discussions about getting along with parents who do not understand you. Parents regularly imagine extreme behavior and complain ("Got to stop this before things get out of hand"), only to find that they have misunderstood the situation. They have projected their thoughts on to behavior without trying to understand the child's point of view. Alas, children sometimes respond to these misunderstandings with "If (s)he thinks I'm doing that then I might as well do that, and really make the blood pressure rise!"

It is commonplace for parents to complain that they never know with whom they will be interacting on a given day. Will the child be fifteen going on forty or fifteen acting like six? On one occasion, the child responds to your distress with comments as perceptive as any a counselor might offer; another time, you are upset and the child is smugly oblivious. The child is sometimes super-responsible about arrangements; at other times there is last-minute confusion. The parent forms the opinion that the child is unreliable and capricious. That is one way of looking at the facts. But it is a mistake to explain behavior in terms of personality traits when the more accurate explanation is that the child is moving towards being perceptive and responsible; she or he is just not quite there yet.

Their children's adolescence is a very difficult time for parents because it calls for skills and attitudes that are little discussed. How do you handle being opposed or ignored by your child? When educators lament the lack of preparation for parenthood, they are not even thinking of preparation for the adolescent years. What preparation does exist is aimed at burping after feedings, preventing diaper rash, and soothing the upset infant. There is no preparation for the child's wearing black nail polish, criticizing your friends, and refusing to go on a family vacation.

The emphasis in the developmental literature is on taking care of and becoming attached to the child. No one tells you that there comes a time when the emphasis will have to be on disengaging. Sure you know in some intellectual way that the child will grow up and leave home, but you are not prepared for the feelings that will accompany this letting go, and for the fact that this period will require you to develop new understandings and ways of relating. It may have taken you a lengthy period of adjustment to care for this child. How can you stop taking care of this child? The answer, of course, involves rethinking what it means to be caring. The old notion of giving care to someone who is dependent on you has to be replaced by a caring that not only tolerates independence, but also glories in it.

When the child seems to be constantly putting you down, what self-respecting person would not resent such treatment? As one mother said to her fourteen-year-old, "I'm glad that I reached this point in my life with the self-esteem that I have, because I feel as if I am losing some every time we speak." You can feel assaulted on all sides. The child thinks your hairdo is dated, your dress is dowdy, your swimming stroke is splashy, your beliefs do not make sense, your friends are all boring, your taste in music is tasteless, your presents are without imagination, and your pronunciation of certain words is incorrect. Telling yourself, "This is just a phase," may not give you patience, but you will feel totally at a loss if you do not realize that this is part of the painful individuation process. Parents will normally feel useless, belittled, and excluded at some times during these years simply because their children are struggling to be self-sufficient, grownup, and separate.

I am not advocating that parents ignore sullen, disrespectful behavior. If you have been hurt by some remark, the best response is not to ignore it. You can say, "I do not know if you meant that remark to hurt the way it did, but you certainly scored a direct hit. What is going on?" If the child wanted to get a rise out of you, an "I'll rise above you" attitude on the part of parents may goad more than it quiets. On the other hand, understanding both that some rebellion is normal at this time and that some remarks may seem more hostile than they really are just because they are unexpected can minimize the overreacting to which parents are prone. They react strongly because they care for their children's good opinion so very much.

Parents may find their children's mood swings difficult, but they may also regard a seeming lack of emotion as even more unbearable. Teenagers frequently strive to be *cool*, which can be interpreted by parents as being cold and uncaring. To be cool is to seem to be in charge of the situation, avant-garde, unflappable. Given the rush of new emotions and many developmental tasks that accompany these years, it is no wonder that the teenager would do everything possible to seem nonchalant and unconcerned. The storm within is sealed over with a glaze of detachment that belies the whirl of thoughts and feelings. It is a mistake to interpret a seeming lack of emotion as indifference or worse; what you see is the outward manifestation of either a struggle to be contained or an inability to get in touch with all those thoughts and feelings.

All the emphasis on the tension-filled quality of these years ignores certain facts. Most teenagers respect their parents' ideas and opinions. They still need their parents very much, but do not want to admit that they do, for such an admission may feel to them like capitulation. Young people want their parents to be committed to them: "Without strong and unambiguous manifestations of parental love, the child or adolescent has little chance of developing self-esteem, constructive and rewarding relationships with others, and a confident sense of his or her own identity."[7] The trouble is that parents are less inclined to show their support and affection when their children seem indifferent to them. Neither generation finds it easy to seem vulnerable.

Adolescents are not necessarily influenced more by peers than by parents, even though friends are very important at this time. Intimacy in the parent-child relationship does not necessarily decline as friendships with peers become more intimate. You can seek psychological closeness with others without valuing less what you already have. Teenagers spend about equal time with parents and peers, but they are engaged in different types of activities with family and friends. In one study, time with parents centered mainly around the completion of a variety of household and social activities (e.g., eating, shopping, performing home chores), though not all time with parents was task-oriented. For example, these adolescents spent about ninety minutes of free time with parents each day, largely watching television together. Mothers and fathers spent about equal time with their children, though they tended to spend more time with the child of the same sex. Children's time with peers, on the other hand, was spent in entertainment, playing games, and talking.[8]

Friends and family may serve different functions, but young people expect the opportunity to dialogue with both. Adolescents value mutual responsiveness in friends, and there is evidence that they prosper most with parents who encourage verbal give-and-take. The quality of the parent-child relationship is shaped by how parents pay attention to their children while they are doing things together.

Obviously not all adolescents are the same. Ages eleven to thirteen are different from fourteen to sixteen and seventeen to nineteen. The most conformist behavior is found earlier;

anxiety concerning friendship peaks in the middle teen years; independence increases in importance as the child reaches late adolescence. Parents are often disturbed by their children's susceptibility to group pressure when they are eleven or twelve. They reason that if the child is already such a conformist, even before she or he is officially a teenager, then the child's adolescence is going to be truly awful. It is a mistake to overgeneralize and to think that matters will only get worse. Behavior tends to be most stilted, exaggerated, stereotyped, and rigid in new situations. Expect some slavish adherence to group fads, but also recognize that such patterned behavior will be modified over time. You may not like aspects of your child at thirteen, but that does not mean things will not have changed by sixteen or seventeen. If you can get over the sense that matters can only get more out of hand, you will feel calmer about dealing with the present. The child is changing too quickly to assume that any eccentric ways will hold forever, even if change seems slow and unnoticeable on any given day.

There are two very different theories of adolescence—one emphasizes disruption, the other continuity. The two viewpoints are not incompatible. This is a transition period and the change process, with its disjointed stops and starts, can leave in its wake an impression of turmoil. That is why you have to keep in mind that change itself is difficult, and not necessarily the child who is changing. The child's move from dependence to independence will end in an interdependence that will make the continuities more obvious over time.

And the child is changing in so many positive ways that get ignored in all the talk about turmoil, crisis, *Sturm and Drang*. She surprises you when you are out of town for a few days by enlisting friends to help in cleaning out a moldy, cluttered, junky garage. She probably would never have done it willingly if it had been expected, but she loved having an opportunity to act the fairy godmother and make an impossible dream come true for you. Your sports-minded son is so serious about taking care of himself that he asks for an iron for Christmas, so he will not be wrinkled during his college days. Who would have ever imagined this domestic side to him a year ago? Your child gets a summer job and tells you about handling a cantankerous customer with a tact of which you are incapable.

Your daughter now knows your taste and has suffficient style herself that she gives your husband excellent ideas about what to buy you for your birthday. You see your son struggle hour after hour to help a friend who has made a suicide attempt, and realize that you have raised an empathetic, perceptive, generous person. Your child experiences failure, manages to put the event into perspective, and bounces back to try again. You ride to the airport with your daughter and find yourself staring at a gorgeous twentyish fellow passenger; he moves out of hearing range, and you say almost in unison, "He is a work of art"—in appreciating him, you appreciate each other in a new way. Your son gives you a thoughtful lecture on the dangers of driving a car that is making awful sounds; he is worried that you are going to get stuck on a deserted street late at night. Your daughter tells you about a speech-contest triumph; she compared samurai warriors to dinosaurs, the judge looked dubious about whether she could bring it off, then told her it was a brilliant comparison when he awarded her a first place. Your child writes you a sentimental note warmly thanking you for all that you did to help get the college applications in on time.

If you are at all reflective, what you learn most by living through your child's adolescence is to develop a better understanding of what you went through when you were that age. My own memory of myself is of a giggly, frenetic girl obsessed with whether anyone but her parents would ever love her. I was annoyed with my parents a good deal of the time. They took my good grades for granted and were overly restrictive, especially since I had never done anything to warrant their concern. That was the trouble. I had never really done anything to write home about, and wondered if I ever would.

I yearned for a future that I could not describe but was convinced that I would never be allowed to leave home and achieve. I felt trapped. I could not even drive a car without my father insisting on being in the car and providing me with a running commentary. How would I ever get away and be me? I saw my life as bounded by dull duties; my mother would talk about the relatives and I had to listen sympathetically, but adults did not ever really listen to me.

They told me what to do and told me what to do; that only made my fantasy life richer. I escaped into books, staring at myself in the mirror, and hibernating in my room. I had energy for everything I wanted to do and was exhausted every time my parents asked me to do something.

I thought of suicide as an answer in case I was never able to get my act together; I was not serious about hurting myself but thought about how everyone would be sorry once I was in my grave. I was the kind of girl every boy's mother liked, but about whom the boys themselves never seemed to get hormonally excited. I thought of becoming a nun—a missionary in a romantic foreign country. I hated the crochet pieces all over the house and imagined surroundings without sauerkraut smells, stuffed furniture, and flowered linoleum. I had a vision of what I could be, if only others would let me be.

I look back now at that girl with great sympathy. I was neither weird nor grotesque, but one version of normal adolescence. Anyone who had told me at the time that I was "normal" would have been attacked, because I wanted to be mysterious, the heroine in a beautifully written story. I look back at my parents with great sympathy and marvel at their tolerance. They did let me have my way more than I realized at the time; they encouraged me to be independent in areas that I find it difficult to let go with my children. The shouting matches with my mother, for which I have never forgiven myself, do not seem as nasty as they once did. I think she understood me without ever saying so. I would like to think that she did not so much see a girl with a big mouth as recognize a series of primal screams.

I look back . . . and I have sympathy for my two teenagers and their friends. Their primal screams do not seem so strident.

· 3 ·

ANXIETY DREAMS

When their children are experiencing adolescence, parents are in the stage of life referred to as middlescence. For some developmentalists, that term encompasses two distinguishable segments: the years from thirty to fifty (Middlescence I) and those from fifty to seventy (Middlescence II). This chapter will focus on the first twenty-year span because most parents are between thirty-five and forty-five, give or take a few years, when their children are adolescents.

What are midlife adults like? They worry about flab, wrinkles, and cholesterol and triglyceride levels. They are either heavily into regular exercise—jogging, racquetball, tennis, swimming, weight lifting, aerobic dance—or they feel guilty about not being involved in some such regular program. When not actually on a diet, they may feel compelled to explain in excruciating detail why they are having dessert at lunchtime (e.g., dinner tonight will be light). They worry about moles that might turn cancerous and gray hair; gray pubic hairs make them feel particularly old. Skin that once was oily now needs layers of cream to make it through the winter. Birthdays are no longer for celebrating.

This is a time when the nurse first asks you during your annual physical, "Do you still have regular periods?" You are insulted by the question. Your child borrows your clothes and looks better in them than you ever have. This is a time when you start thinking twice about shoveling heavy snow and walking on ice. This is a time when you meet a handsome young man and think, He ought to meet my daughter, then want to cry. This is a time when you start reading the obituary column regularly and become numbers conscious. Ruffles and doodads that once looked smart on you now look silly—too young for you. How can you think of going back to school yourself when your child's college is going to cost a small fortune?! You feel like a "has-been," without ever having "been."

Where once you could drink into the wee hours of the morning and make it to work on time with little sleep, two martinis and you can feel them. And they do not feel good! Where once you loved to go driving on weekends just for fun, getting behind the wheel is a chore because the commute to and from work is so long. You are more involved in funerals and divorces than in marriages and christenings. Where once you had lavish, sensual dreams, now most that you remember have anxiety as their theme: airplane connections missed; someone is chasing you; work is overdue; intimations of death.

You once thought that you would write "the great American novel," now doubt if you ever will. You tell your favorite story for the hundredth time and are bored with hearing it again. A dear friend has died of cancer, and he was not much older than you are. You feel unappreciated at the office. You wonder if the next career move will ever come your way, and if it does, are you really prepared to move to another city? You feel too tired to start all over finding a new barber, church, delicatessen, tailor, and garage mechanic.

Words evade you, and you start worrying about memory loss, brain tumors, and Alzheimer's disease. You are forever making arrangements for elderly relations; you joke about opening your own nursing home, but dealing with parents who do not remember your name is no laughing matter. A parent dies, and you feel moved up in line. You go to bed before your children do; you need your rest. You would rather eat or watch a movie at home; it's easier than going out. You have more sympathy for Shakespeare's *King Lear* than his *Romeo and Juliet*. Your daughter glances sideways at her bust line, and you are reminded that you are over thirty-five and should have a mammogram; you cannot be too careful about detecting breast cancer.

It seems to take longer to shake the flu when you get it. Ads for baldness and arthritis cures are read more carefully. You now know what your mother meant when she complained of "stiffness." The grudges you once held about how you were raised have lost their punch; you realize that you have not given your parents full credit for being as savvy and tolerant as they were. You feel dated because you can remember when bacon, eggs, coffee with saccharin, and a cigarette afterwards while sunbathing represented the good life; you now see the good life fraught with carcinogenic agents. Planning for your retirement now has an urgency about it.

The child for whom you had to slow down so he could keep up, now slows down his pace for you. Your wife says there is a new young man at the office, and you wonder how old he is. These days "young" encompasses quite a span—anyone your age or younger. Your notion of "old" has changed, too; it starts at eighty. The towels that you got as a wedding present are threadbare. Authority figures—clergy, military, police, physicians—seem to be getting younger and younger. Mail means bills and phone calls mean someone wants something from you; they both once meant keeping in touch with friends. You look and sound like your parents more and more. You and your partner seem locked into having the same conversations over and over again. Lovemaking is routine.

Though these characterizations are skewed in a negative direction, they do conjure up, in a superficial way, some of the issues of this period. Many of the same issues that preoccupy the teenager also concern her or his parents, but there is a sense in which the generations seem to be moving in opposite directions. Teenagers are coming to terms with their sexuality; their parents are worried about staying vital, sensual, and attractive. Teenagers feel complimented when they are mistaken for being older than their years; their parents feel complimented when they are mistaken for being younger than their years. Teenagers are learning how to drive and contemplating what it means to drink, whereas their parents may be disenchanted with both. The children can eat enormous amounts of food during this growth spurt and not gain weight; the parents eat less than they once did and still gain weight. The young people are delighting in their newfound cognitive abilities, as their parents worry about their own brain cells misfiring in all directions.

Both generations peer into the mirror a great deal; teenagers search for the perfect hairdo, while their parents count gray hairs and measure bald spots. The children can abuse their bodies without obvious ill effects; their parents pamper their bodies but the results are mixed. Teenagers are worried about finding themselves; their parents are concerned about losing what they have worked so hard to get. Both generations are in a period of heightened introspection, but this stocktaking is an evaluation of promises realized for the parents, whereas the children are just figuring out what promise they have. The children have open to them a world of possibilities; the parents wonder, Is that all there is? They feel boxed in by choices already made.

This sense of switching places can be very strong. The mother anticipates the end of her reproductive capabilities just when her daughter may be starting hers. The son's potency seems boundless just when the father may be having some problems with impotence. As E. James Anthony has noted:

> It is clear that psychologically speaking the adolescent is on his way up when the caretaking adults are on their way down. This basic anabolic-catabolic distinction understandably provokes in the adult envy for the adolescent's youthful vigor with all its freedom, freshness, and joyful foolishness.[1]

There is envy, and sometimes it is a bit foolish when it leads to competitive games on a Sunday afternoon.

The adults are developing a different time perspective. It is now clear to the parents that time is finite; they start thinking in terms of time-left-to-live. Teenagers, of course, see themselves as having practically all the time in the world. The heroine of the movie *Rachel, Rachel* said when she was thirty-five that that was her last ascending summer. Adolescents want to move on, but their midlife parents do not find the future all that attractive.

I have painted a bleak picture, but the issues of both adolescence and middlescence have in common a tendency to be negative when discussed at a stereotypic level. This time has many positive features, but they are not as obvious at first glance. Midlife adults are the powers that be in any society—the managers, bosses, officers, consultants, negotiators, advisors, mentors, and sponsors. They are moving into top leadership positions, have economic clout, and often are the support of both the younger generation and the older one. The awkwardness of youth has been replaced by a mellow sureness. So long as life has not been too hard on the individual, experience can make the face more interesting. There is a confidence and authority about them that is impossible to achieve when you are young. Instead of worrying about pleasing others, they concentrate more on pleasing themselves. They are coming fully into their own. They can juggle an assortment of family, work, and community involvements that would have exhausted them at the age of twenty. These women and men are at their peak. They have more money, savvy, responsibilities, and character than ever before, but being at the peak makes them worry all the more about the slide down. Their children look to the future, but the parents want to hold it back because they think it means their downgrading.

Freudians have described both puberty and the climacteric in terms of a storm of instincts. The genital impulses that played such a role in shaping the behavior of the adolescent are thought to flare up again in anticipation of a decline in physical sexual function. This is a time when both sexes think in terms of having one last big fling before they are too unattractive to capture a lover's attention. Their quests have become a staple of the personals: Mischievous and attractive, midlife woman seeks nice, non-smoking man with sense of humor . . . Mischief-making, slightly married man in fifth decade has much to offer a woman in her third or fourth . . . Full-bodied, full-flavored, full of life woman (41) seeks fulfilling relationship.

There is a long tradition associating reproductive ability with growth and loss of reproductive ability with decline. Yet recent data on general intellectual capacity, perceptual processes, creativity, sexual activity, and problem-solving ability demonstrate that diminished capacity is not the rule come middle adulthood. The body improves *after* the teenage years: "Until middle age, there is evidence that the brain continues to show increasing nerve insulation, or what neurologists call myelinization."[2] Such maturation may facilitate more integrated modes of social response. Lillian E. Troll found that development continues well past middle age: "It is far from inevitable that we must get dumber as we get older. In fact, it is possible to get a lot wiser."[3] Losses of speed and sensory acuity can be more than balanced by increases in deliberation and experience.

Robert C. Peck sees four possible advantages to this period: Physique-based values give way to wisdom-based values; socializing becomes more important than sexualizing so individual personality takes on greater meaning; greater emotional flexibility can lead to a more varied, differentiated set of relationships than ever before; greater mental flexibility can lead to having an increased sense of mastery over one's experience.[4] This is the prime of life—"the period of maximum capacity and ability to handle a highly complex environment and a highly differentiated self."[5] One's sense of identity is consolidated. So long as the individual does not become mired in despair, this can be a time of self-awareness, selectivity, mastery, breadth, competence, a wide array of cognitive strategies, structuring and restructuring of experience, conceptual complexity, toleration for ambiguity, respect for individuality, self-fulfillment, manipulation and control of the environment. Individuals can become "more compassionate, more reflective and judicious, less tyrannized by inner conflicts and external demands, and more genuinely loving."[6]

The tasks of the middle years are many:

1. Developing socioeconomic consolidation;
2. Evaluating one's occupation or career in light of a personal value system;
3. Helping younger persons (e.g., biologic offspring) to become integrated human beings;
4. Enhancing or redeveloping intimacy with spouse or most significant other;
5. Developing a few deep friendships;
6. Helping aging persons (e.g., parents or in-laws) progress through the later years of life;
7. Assuming responsible positions in

occupational, social, and civic activities,
organizations, and communities;

8. Maintaining and improving the home or other
   forms of property;
9. Using leisure time in satisfying and creative
   ways;
10. Adjusting to biologic or personal system
    changes that occur.[7]

As a whole, the tasks involve a continued expansion of interests rather than any diminution. In a real sense, the individual is getting better. The individual is no longer "driven," but finds herself or himself "in the driver's seat."

Given Jack Benny's mythic reluctance to get older than thirty-nine, all in American society are bound to wonder if there is life after forty and what it looks like. External events, such as work opportunities, the decline of a parent, and the child leaving home, can serve as catalysts for the rethinking that occurs during this time. For example, the task of socioeconomic consolidation will take on a greater intensity following a divorce, as will developing a few good friendships. But some developmentalists hold that the stocktaking which characterizes this time of life is a function of just reaching a particular age.

Daniel Levinson believes that stable periods ordinarily last six or seven years, then "the life structure that has formed the basis for stability comes into question and must be modified."[8] For him, the "settling down" to invest themselves in work, family, and whatever else is important that characterized the thirties for men is bound to be rethought at midlife. Men of this age ask, "What have I done with my life? What is it I truly want? Where am I headed?" After this time of reappraisal and exploration, a new life structure is pieced together that corrects for any perceived imbalance. The individual develops a firmer sense of what matters the most to him. He becomes increasingly concerned about what his legacy to the future will be. In becoming concerned about this legacy, he may become more engaged in the lives of his children.

Gail Sheehy also believes that the settling down which characterized the early thirties for women gives way to a "my last chance" urgency around thirty-five.[9] It is only at thirty-five or thereabouts that women "find it possible to free themselves from a triple bind: dependency on mother, dependency on husband, and bondage to their children."[10] They are free to ask what they are beyond their mother's daughter, husband's wife, and children's mother. The woman wonders where she is going in her family life and/or career. Should she break out of the rut she is in . . . finish her education . . . take a new job . . . remarry . . . get divorced? What follows is the deadline decade— "seeing the dark first, disassembling ourselves, then glimpsing the light, and regathering our parts into a renewal."[11] The woman comes to realize that she cannot live through anyone else, child or husband; the influence you exert in life is through what you become yourself. This may be her last chance to become truly her own person.

For both sexes, the stable patterns of the twenties and early thirties give way to a period of active psychological change between thirty-five and forty. Those who are married become less satisfied with their marriages: "They feel weary of devoting themselves to the task of being what they are supposed to (although they continue on), and just want to be what they are."[12] They feel squeezed by time pressures, but feel that there is still time to make some dreams come true if they hurry. In this reworking of old dreams, some are abandoned as outmoded fantasies and some become the basis for rededicating their lives. By fifty, they will have more of a sense that the "die is cast," and that can be a relief. They will have come to know and to appreciate themselves for what they are; they may give up trying to change the spouse in favor of accepting her or him. They will also come to value their spouses more.

During the midlife transition, individuals become concerned about encouraging in themselves those aspects of personality that have been hitherto least developed. If a woman has immersed herself in homemaking and childrearing, then she is likely to become more interested in developing her occupational side. If a man has been immersed in his job, then he is likely to become more concerned with developing his nurturing and artistic side. Instead of wondering what it means to be a woman or a man (one of the tasks of adolescence), the midlife individual becomes concerned about what it means to be a full human being. How do you combine inside yourself the best of stereotypes and become, in the process, your own person— that is, gentle *and* assertive, independent *and* people-oriented, creative *and* careful, expressive *and* self-contained?

This time of ferment has consequences for parenting. Going through their own identity crisis can leave parents too exhausted to want to deal with their children's emotional turmoil. As they question the choices that they have made, they can appear jaded and disgruntled just when their children need them to be optimistic and excited about their plans. The parents' opinions about their past may leave them overly opinionated about what is best for their children's future. The parents' hurts may leave them urging caution all the time. If the parents are not satisfied with themselves, this may leave them always unsatisfied with their children.

The parent who feels personally confused may opt out of much involvement on the grounds that you cannot help anyone else before you know yourself. The mother who worries that no one takes her seriously because she has never had a career of her own may be predisposed to see every rebellious gesture as a personal affront rather than as a part of the process of growing up. The mother who wants her life to be more than drudgery may resent all those moments when her child is far from enjoyable. The self-centered father confronting the self-centered child may be more prepared to do battle than to listen. The newly divorced father may be so caught up with his sexual freedom that he spends less and less time with his son; he does not want to be labeled old enough to have a child of that age. The stepmother concerned with making a second marriage work may resent her teenage stepdaughter's censorious comments and refer to her always as bitch-goddess; her own concerns about being accepted limit her ability to be sympathetic to the child's concerns about the same issue.

As teenagers spend more and more time away from home, they want home to remain a set place to come back to, but their parents may be thinking this is their last chance to do something different. They change, their children react, and both sides are surprised by the intensity of their feelings. The mother rethinking her options may feel in a state of suspended animation, and become remote from her children. The child thinks, No one understands me, and the father is not able to make the effort to understand because he is thinking the same thing about his situation. Both generations feel sealed off from each other by misunderstandings that have piled up to form invisible walls. The child wants to talk and be listened to, as does the parent; instead of connecting, they may engage in parallel play. Since this is a time of reevaluation, the parent may be wondering whether she or he should have had children. This very question, even when it is unspoken, can have a distancing effect on parent-child exchanges. In this time of reappraisal, children are all the more regarded as reflections of their parents' worth; any negative qualities in the child may be seen as "Ds" on the parent's report card. That is a heavy burden to put on any relationship.

Women may feel particularly beset at this time. As one mother said, "God so loved women that *He* gave them menopause, aging parents, and adolescent children all at the same time." Just when the woman wants to be able to come into her own, she may find herself weighed down by new problems and a growing sense that she is over the hill. To the extent that she has immersed herself in home and family, it may be especially difficult to deal with the teenager who says in every word and deed, "I am not a baby anymore." The woman starts the quest for the postponed self, and may become more unavailable to her children for the conversation and affirmation that they need from her. Because she is so immersed in her own thoughts and feelings, her responses to her children may be rote: "There's a spot on your shirt; change into a new one . . . You need to make an appointment with the dentist . . . Stop slouching . . . Stop picking your face. . . ."

The woman sees the child becoming increasingly self-reliant and may be reminded of her own lack of self-confidence. The child does not need her in the old way, and that becomes a metaphor for her life—"No one needs me." The "empty nest" transition is not the universal problem it was once thought to be for women, but it can be a "trigger event" for women with other significant problems. For some middle-aged women, it can be a time of low life satisfaction, pessimism, existential despair, and negative feelings towards their husbands. The middle-aged woman who wants to grow and develop, but who can see no way to do so, is most likely to be distressed. She may look ahead to years devoid of any promise of personal accomplishment; the only things she can look forward to are her children's high school graduation, their marriage, their children, and her husband's retirement. Looking at her children and their distress, she may feel even more distressed herself because there is an emotional cost to caring. The greater investment of women in the lives of those around them leaves them vulnerable when others experience undesirable life events, and all teenagers have some troubles.

The woman who has been non-traditional may also have special problems at this time. Though she has been unswervingly committed to developing her own career for years, she may now have serious second thoughts about whether she did the right thing in combining work and family. These pangs of guilt appear whenever her children seem distressed, which probably means several times each week. Even though being a woman who "does it all" is applauded only when nothing obvious goes wrong, she may still be surprised by the ferocity of her doubts when her child seems remote or rebellious. She may feel unreasonably to blame; she may also be very angry because mothers continue to feel responsible for what they cannot control.

The non-traditional woman may have embarked on motherhood with feminist analyses of the role to guide her. Since none of this literature focuses on the experience of a mother with teenagers, she has nothing to hold on to in helping her to understand this period of her life. Moreover, the feminist literature has tended to be critical of the relationship between mother and adult daughter. Almost all feminists identify with the daughter striking out on her own rather than the mother being left behind. Now that she has a child moving away from her, the feminist may feel lost. Being a non-traditional woman heretofore was associated with rebellion, vigor, and youth. Suddenly, her daughter is the one who is rebellious, vigorous, and young. The mother has become the older woman, and positive images of the older woman remain to be written, so she feels at odds with the situation. Is she now what she has previously railed against?

At midlife, the shift for men is often from an emphasis on work to a greater investment in family and private life. Up until that time individual achievement may have been the standard of self-assessment and success. Whereas traditional women may be absorbed in worrying about whether life has left them behind when their children grow up, traditional men may now regret all those times when they were too busy to spend time with their children. Preoccupied with these regrets, they may be more caught up with what they did not do when the child was six than prepared to deal with the reality of a sixteen-year-old. When you feel that you have to make up for what you did not do before, your orientation is to providing the affection and attention that the young child needs, not to providing the space that the older child wants. Parents have a tendency to become nostalgic about the past at this point. As they rethink where they have been, the period when their children were young may strike them as having been a golden time. They remember not how piercing the cry could be, but how adorable the baby was, full of gurgling sounds, sweet smells, and velvety touches. The things that once grated on the nerves now seem cute. Toilet training seems easy compared to dealing with a moody teenager. Young children think the world of their parents, and that is an enviable position in which to be. As parents put the past into perspective, history gets, if not rewritten, at least sanitized. The blood, sweat, and tears are cleaned away, and an image emerges that is picture perfect. Some are so taken with a past that now seems halcyon that they decide to have one last fling at youth and have another baby.

This rethinking is occasioned by the stocktaking the parents are doing. When they think back, they are conscious of possibilities lost: If they only had it to do again, this time they would do everything right. They would know how to handle a crying infant, a pouty four-year-old, a curious eight-year-old. Some of their parents' reminiscing is important to adolescents, for they, too, are rethinking where they have been. As parents reflect back on the antics of their child at a younger age, that child is usually made to feel that he was impish, lovable, and clever. When you are no longer a baby, it is good to have that part of you squared away: "I sure was adorable then." You can proceed into the future optimistically, knowing that your past was well done.

There is a danger, though, that parents, uncomfortable with the present state of affairs, may talk about the past so much that they inadvertently communicate displeasure with the child in the present. The chubby teenager who is told over and over again how tiny she was at birth may feel that her parents are really saying, "But look at you now!" The shy boy who is repeatedly reminded of how he used to think nothing about walking up to strangers and engaging them in conversation may believe that his parents wish that he had never grown up. Too much of "Where did my beautiful little girl (boy) go?" and teenagers can become convinced that they are not loved for what they now are. Of course, what the parents are really wondering is, What has happened to them?

Teenagers are very worried about whether their parents will continue to love them and to support them as they stop looking like a child. Can they still hold their parents' affection even though the terms of the relationship are changing? To the extent that parents are obviously nostalgic about the past, how can the children move towards the future? What is more, the parents are not so much nostalgic about the lived past as they are wistful about what they now think they could do with the same set of opportunities.

Not only are parents rethinking their children's early years, but this is also a time when parents generally indulge in many fantasies about youth:

> If complaint about adolescent children forms a staple of middle-class, middle-aged conversation, such complaint often contains undertones of admiration or even awe. . . . The parental generation see intelli-

gence, strength, sexual energy, all reaching a high pitch in the postpuberty years. They see youth's suffering, too, but consider it a small price to pay.[13]

Myths of youth capture the adult imagination: ". . . young people have all the fun, and, far worse, they outlive us."[14]

Adolescence is, in a way, society's favorite age. Pubescent beauty is used to sell a variety of products from jeans to cars. Adults envy the young their sense of aliveness. Teenagers, with their passions and longings, are romantic creatures—the stuff of which many a novel has been written by middle-aged authors. The young are not hemmed in by responsibilities, but have open to them unlimited possibilities. They represent Paradise Lost.

The middle-aged do see that they have improved over time. They have some sense of finally coming into their own. They think that they now could handle adolescence well. If they could go back in time, they would hold on longer to the muscles of youth, make better choices, and take advantage of every opportunity that came their way. It has taken them this long to get the hang of things; now they would know how to handle a sixteen-year-old body with respect. It is not that these adults would gladly switch places with their children, but there is that bittersweet sense of youth being wasted on the young.

This sense that they are finally ready to handle adolescence with style leaves the middle-aged likely to carp when their child does not seem to be doing a good job of being a teenager: How can that child miss that opportunity? You bemoan how oblivious the child seems to be, and it is true. The child cannot see what you see because it took many years *past* adolescence for you to get to the point where you are now. This point cannot be overstated. You are inclined to be annoyed when your child cannot combine brawn and brains, energy and direction, creativity and patience the way you are finally prepared to do.

Alas, the children can do, but cannot see, what their parents can see, but cannot necessarily do.

You may be all the more annoyed because you see the child as privileged at this time of life in a way that you were not: When you were this age, you did not have parents willing to spend thousands of dollars on your teeth. . . . When you were this age, even going out for a hamburger was a special treat. . . . When you were this age, you did not have parents who paid so much attention to you. . . . When you were this age, you did not have a closet full of pretty clothes. . . . You think that you would have turned out better if you had only had the kind of parenting this child has, and are annoyed that the child is not properly appreciative. The child's appreciation, or lack thereof, is not what is ultimately bothering you. You are in a period of rethinking, and one of the major tasks is to stop mourning what you are not and to appreciate what you are.

You want to feel appreciated for all the obvious reasons, but also because this is a period when you are often dealing with elderly parents. You confront your own sense of filial responsibility and wonder how much your children will care for you as you grow older. Because teenagers can be so self-centered at times, you imagine them as ingrates who will never bother to visit you. If at some future time you cannot do for them, will they ever do anything for you? Many of your feelings have less to do with your children's behavior than with the self-pity you are feeling, occasioned by the stocktaking. Alas, the more you feel sorry for yourself and remind your children of how ungrateful they are, the more you can feel isolated. The children cannot figure out where you are coming from. That, of course, is what you have to figure out: Where are you coming from?

Though some of the dynamics of this period can add to tensions between the generations, it is to the teenager's advantage to have middle-aged parents. Seeing middle-aged parents struggle with their own identity problems can be comforting to teenage children who worry about making the "right" choices; their parents are proof positive that you can always rethink options. As parents remember their awkward past, it helps children to know that they did not always see themselves as finished products. When you are trying to get clear about what you believe, it helps to talk matters over with individuals who can see that most issues are complicated, not merely either/or decisions. The parent who has mellowed with age can reassure the child that she was not always as sure of herself as she now seems to be. A parent's regrets, so long as they do not turn into ugly recriminations, can energize the child to make the most of opportunities. Middle-aged, you can admit failures that once were unspeakable, and become an object lesson to your child.

Being middle-aged, you have learned to put matters into a context. You no longer have as strong an opinion as you once did on the best place to live, the smartest job to have, the ideal person to love. Life is what you make of it; there are pros and cons to every choice. Your own parents were neither saints nor devils, but people limited by their piece of time, just as you are. One argument need not mean the end of a relationship; long-term relationships go through cycles of good times and bad. You can live with ambiguities because you can appreciate a variety of opinions; in many situations, there are no right or wrong answers. This middle-aged sense of perspective is needed by the teenager for whom life is so intense that balance is difficult to achieve.

On the other hand, being with teenagers can help the parents through a difficult period. Being able to relate to the younger generation can reassure you that you are not out of touch with things. Every time you help your child put feelings into words, you understand yourself better, too. All those times when you are convinced that you have not gotten very far in life dissolve when you can see that you are in a very different spot from your children. Compared to them, you do not worry so much about having friends because you have a few who have been a comfort through thick and thin. You do not worry so much about your looks because some friends who were the body-beautiful types as teens have not worn as well as you have. You do not worry so much about whether you are smart because other things are just as important to success as brains—perseverance, hard work, creativity, a sense of humor. You do not worry so much about doing the right thing because unexpected and unwanted things have happened in your life that have turned out for the best. You understand what it means to write straight with crooked lines!

You also know that your job is to help your soon-to-be-adult child learn how to write straight with crooked lines.

· 4 ·

THE PHYSICAL
WORK IS
OVER, BUT . . .

By the time you reach the second decade of parenthood, you expect the brunt of parenting to be over. The main burden should be over, because children of this age can already dress and bathe themselves, read directions, and manage the daily routine of school. They not only can meet most of their personal needs, but also regularly help out around the house. Sure, they may need to be reminded of chores to be done and these responsibilities are not always assumed without some grumbling and muttering, but competence has clearly taken the place of constant needfulness. Not only are baby-sitters not necessary every time you set foot out the door, but the child of ten, eleven, or twelve may be already earning some money amusing the toddler in the house up the street.

As a parent, you are delighted with your child's newfound skills. Diapers, swooping into a locked mouth with a spoonful of strained plums, and frequent shrill cries are part of the past. You come across an electrical outlet stopped with a plastic plug and regard it as an anachronism—something out of historical time. Instead of needing help with the child, you get help from your child. The standards of cleanliness may not be yours, but the offer is sincere, and the quality promises to improve with practice. As a psychologically astute parent, you know that constant criticism can nip enthusiasm in the bud, so you tolerate sprays of flour and sugar on the floor as you bake together.

You are delighted with this child who can now do so much: draw detailed pictures, visit an elderly neighbor, handle an allowance, shovel snow, bag garbage, play team sports, practice the piano, amuse your parents when they visit. Parenting is not without problems. There are afternoons of non-stop bickering, messy rooms, a taste for junk food, not remembering to feed the dog, helter-skelter hygiene, grades that do not reflect the child's potential. Still, you probably can live with most of the child's faults because this is a time when the child can be a fun companion. You can dine at a restaurant and not have to worry that your child is going to turn over everything within reach or scream for attention.

As a parent, you may feel pleased with yourself. You no longer fall apart every time the child has an earache, because you know how to proceed. You may even give advice at the office when another father worries about his child having an imaginary friend. You urge tolerance because you remember when your daughter had an invisible pal named Amanda who always got her into trouble. You feel capable and tolerant compared to how you used to be.

You are also beginning to feel free in a way that you have missed these last few years. You no longer feel so "on call" as a parent, and have more time for yourself and your partner. If you set aside your own career interests during the child's early years, you may be in the process of getting back in the job market or returning to school for some retooling. If your work life was modified by some sense that you needed to combine career and family so the children did not lose out, you may be thinking that this is the time to push career because family life is finally stable. After all, you have only so many years left to get where you want to go!

You are ready to move in a new direction because things seem relatively stable. The physical work of parenting is largely over, even though your financial responsibilities are not, and that may be why you feel a desire to get reinvested in the world of work. The child still needs some framework for getting clean clothes, nutritious meals, and rides all over town (to ballet classes, flute lessons, football games, tennis matches, friends' homes, the shopping mall, movies, etc.), but the child can contribute to this structure by helping with laundry, cooking, and arranging rides. You know that the child has emotional needs, too, but even in that department matters appear even-keeled. The child seems reasonably well adjusted (temper is more controlled, friendships are blossoming); you feel attached to the child (you cannot imagine life without this child). You are no fool; you know that relationships need upkeep. Still and all, you feel that most of the difficult moments of parenting are behind rather than ahead of you. This viewpoint may leave you unprepared for the work of the second decade of parenthood.

For all the bad press teenagers have received, many parents are still unprepared to deal with the tensions that go with those years. In part, this is because parents tend to be literal-minded: They do not expect teenage behavior before the child is thirteen years old, and children can change dramatically before then. Parents also hope that it will be different with them. Others may experience stress and strain during those years, but many parents assume that the equilibrium they personally established by the time the child was ten years old will hold thereafter. This child who has already mastered so much will easily master what comes next because a firm foundation exists. The assumption is that rebellious behavior comes only to those parents who, in some sense, ask for it.

There is enormous emphasis in the childrearing literature on the importance of the early years. The prevailing opinion is that if you meet the needs of the young child you will have given the child a foundation for life. Be available to the toddler, and you will not have toddler-like behavior showing up when the child is fourteen years old. Most parents, when pressed, would admit that there is a limit to how much filling early needs for acceptance, nurturance, stimulation, and guidance can meet later needs for independence, assertiveness, and self-expression, but parents hear so much about the importance of beginnings that they easily err on the side of underestimating the adjustments necessary later. They may even assume that those who experience difficulties during the child's teenage years, by definition, did not spend enough quality time with the child in the early years.

Society conspires to make parenting seem relatively easy in the child's second decade. The mother who does not work outside the home may be automatically regarded as lazy: Why doesn't she do something useful now that her children are practically grown and she has so much time on her hands? To spend considerable time being involved with your children at this point may be interpreted by some as mollycoddling: Doesn't she know when to let go? The "letting go" quality of these years is frequently equated with distancing, becoming less involved. You are expected to have more time available. Friends may even suggest that you spend more time with your partner and less time with your children: "They're going to be gone soon, and then what will you do?" In a thousand different ways, you are psyched up for less parenting rather than more, for less intense feelings rather than greater intensity. You are then unprepared for the reality of the situation.

The advice, of course, is partially correct. You no longer

have to worry so much about the child's play environment being free of hazards or to keep the child within visual range. The problem is that you, and others, act as if the child's second decade of development is facilitated by not doing (or doing less of) what you have been doing all along, rather than by doing something new. But you are, in fact, into something new.

The childrearing literature does relatively little to prepare you for this something new, since it focuses largely on establishing bonds, not on letting go of old ways of relating. Those few models that have an over-time perspective do not develop the issues of this period at any length. Joan Aldous describes the five stages of family development in terms of (a) the establishment stage (time of marriage), (b) the expanding stage (addition of first child to arrival of last one), (c) the stable stage (period of childrearing until first child leaves home), (d) the contracting stage (period when children are leaving home until last child has gone), and (e) the couple-alone stage (the focus is back on being a couple rather than on parenting).[1] This model suggests that an expansion of parenting is followed by some stability, then by contraction. Even though this theorist is emphasizing changes in the size of the family and is not focusing on changes in psychological themes over time, you are still likely to be ill prepared for "more" at adolescence when such terminology is used.

Saul L. Brown has conceptualized a family development task cycle.[2] Task 1 is establishing basic commitment. Task 2 is creating a system for mutual nurturance. Task 3 involves defining mechanisms for mutual encouragement of individuation and autonomy. Task 4 is facilitating ego mastery. Though the tasks are not linked specifically to the age of the child, parents are told that being direct and authoritative is particularly important in dealing with adolescents. Discussing the clinical implications of the fourth task, Brown insists that parents stand up to the adolescent even though it is easier to do this in the earlier phases of the family cycle. The emphasis is on taking a firm stand with blustering adolescents, which suggests that the child, but not necessarily the parent, is acting in a different way.

Robert Selman outlines five levels in parent-child relations.[3] During the period of egotistic understanding, children understand parents only as bosses (Level 0); eventually children begin to conceive of parents as caretakers and helpers (Level 1). The conception of the parent as "guidance counselor–need satisfier" characterizes Level 2. Level 3 coincides with adolescence; parent and child mutually show tolerance and respect. By Level 4, there is recognition that parent-child relations change as the circumstances, abilities, and needs of each change. This model does not emphasize stability and contraction, and leaves one more prepared for conflict. Getting along during the teenage years is characterized not by absolute agreement but by respect for each other's position. Conflicts between obedience to parents and the needs of growing children for autonomy and independence are addressed. Still, even this model's emphasis on growing mutuality may leave you unprepared for the parent's having to act in an appreciably new way.

To the extent that the traditional view of adolescence has emphasized the breaking-away process in which the child gradually moves away from the family, the major function of the parents during this developmental phase would seem to be to give the child someone to leave. But in fact parents play a much more central role during this time than is typically acknowledged. The child, in the process of becoming individuated, needs parents as active agents in the construction of an independent self. In order to fashion a mature individual, the parents must treat the child as an individual capable of independent, responsible behavior. The primary bond between parent and child is transformed, not abandoned. The adolescent becomes her or his own person through interactions with family members.

For the adolescent to become her or his own person, parenting must change in several respects. The principal change is that it becomes less instrumental and expressive, and more responsive. Instead of doing for the child, the parent encourages the child to do for herself or himself. You move away from making decisions for the child to helping the child learn the decision-making process. There are relatively few concrete tasks that now require the parents to take charge of the situation. For example, you do not have to shop for clothes because your son is increasingly able to choose for himself. What is more, he has definite tastes that may or may not coincide with your own. You can reserve the right to set limits on price or specify minimum standards, but the child needs leeway to develop his own style. You can respond to his decision-making process (e.g., complimenting his choice, remarking on the upkeep problems of certain fabrics), but you can no longer act as if the child has to be dressed by you.

What is true of clothes is true of many other things, for example, course schedules, leisure activities, and involvement in sports. If you tell your daughter what to do, she will either resent your pushing and resist your suggestions, or she will accept your viewpoint without learning how to form her own judgments. That does not mean that the parent does not have a say, but you have to remember that it is only one say. You can remind her of courses needed for college, the advantages and disadvantages of study halls, the companionship she will miss by not joining clubs, how boxed in she will be playing varsity basketball *and* keeping up with the swim team. But you are responding to her agenda rather than setting one of your own. This does not mean that you cannot urge your perspective—and, indeed, you have a responsibility to do just that—but you have to recognize that you cannot cry wolf too many times. You have to reserve speeches about dire consequences for those times when they are definitely warranted. If you push your opinion on everything, you only convey that you are obstinate, and that may make her mulish in turn. If you are always spouting your convictions, then specific positions do not stand out; your beliefs become only background noise.

It is important to recognize that the decision-making takes place within a need for some experimentation. The child is eager to try on different ideas in order to see if they fit his style. If he had all decisions made for him, he would feel like a puppet instead of a real person. Like Pinocchio, the child needs to make some wrong decisions in order to learn what a mistake it is to go in certain directions. But parents are used to making decisions and taking the consequences, and are not sure that they want to live with the consequences of their children's decisions. You are never sure of how much responsibility the child should assume at any given moment, on the way to the time when the child will be totally responsible for her or his actions. It can feel ego-deflating to become only a resource instead of being the final word on any subject.

Not only are there fewer concrete tasks parents have to perform, but the expressive dimension of parenting also has to be reconceptualized. With the young child, you can equate daily caresses with successful parenting. Routine embraces may be dismissed by the adolescent as just another aspect of meaningless expectations. The parent who was once encouraged to cuddle the child may have come to expect goodnight kisses; they represent an affectionate tie. On the other hand, the child resists anything that smacks of obeisance and does not want her or his feelings to be scheduled by anyone else. Kisses and hugs have to be spontaneous, not demanded.

Children want emotional connections, but they also wish to be loved for what they are in the present. The parent who regularly says, "I love you," but then responds to the child's expressed feelings with pious platitudes will be challenged: "How can you love me when you don't really bother to know me?" Of course, the parent may respond with anger—"That's preposterous; I have known you all your life"—without hearing between the lines. The child does not want empty words, meaningless gestures, or routine expectations. This is a time when he wants to rethink what has heretofore been taken for granted, and not be anyone's lapdog.

This is not to say that children do not want hugs and kisses. They appreciate them most when they are not formalities—"Remember to kiss Aunt Jane hello"—but are impromptu. Is Aunt Jane willing to put her arms spontaneously around a niece making a personal statement by spiked hair with blue tips, twenty black plastic bracelets, and as many unmatched earrings as the earlobes can hold? The "don't touch me" moments are not meant to communicate "leave me alone forever," but that the ground rules are changing.

The switch in emphasis can be difficult for parents to accomplish. It is easier to do something yourself than to work with someone else as she or he struggles to do something you can already do with ease. It is easier to do concrete things (e.g., give money, schedule activities) than to listen attentively to thoughts and feelings. It is easier to rely on routine embraces than to leave yourself open to the rejection of your spontaneous hugs. Parents are used to being in control; they may think that it is essential if anything is to be done. Being in control makes them feel indispensable; being their child's sounding board may make them feel dispensable. Telling someone else what to do confirms you as an authority; responding to someone else's framework makes you feel of secondary importance.

There is a tendency for some parents to think, If you want to have it your way, then go ahead and have it your way, and to opt out of the exchange. If they cannot be the assumed authority they abrogate all responsibility. If adolescents disagree they are treated as disagreeable and allowed to flounder. That will teach them! Sometimes, adults tend to let adolescents be the sole arbiters of what is best for them without providing them with the view from their vantage point. This tendency may be due to the difficulty parents have in conceptualizing authority without being authoritarian. If they cannot be the acknowledged authority then they do not bother.

Not only does parenting have less of a "hands-on" quality during the second decade of parenthood, but there are also no longer neat beginnings and endings to what you do. When the task was to change a diaper, you had a sweet-smelling baby to show for all the washing and powdering that you did. Keep the child company while he watches *Sesame Street*, reinforce that "J" comes before "K," get your child to sing the alphabet song while taking a bath, and there will come a time when you can proudly announce to the grandparents that he knows his letters. When the objective was getting your daughter to learn how to swim, all you had to do was drive her every Tuesday and Thursday to the local YMCA as she made her way over the months from polliwog to shark. The tasks of the first decade of parenthood are time-consuming, but you have much to show for your efforts. There are concrete accomplishments that you can name.

The tasks of the second decade of parenthood are time-consuming, too, but you usually do not have something obvious to show for your efforts. For example, you are writing a report that is due the next day, and your son sits down. After some pleasantries are exchanged, you realize that he is a bit on edge. You decide to be direct: "Is something bothering you?" He denies that that is the case, and asks you about a photograph that you have on your desk. You are pressed for time, but have a hunch that he is testing you: Will you bother with him, even though you are fidgeting with papers?

You push on. "You say that nothing is bothering you, but I

am not convinced. Can I help you in any way?" Your son says, "It's nothing much," then slowly proceeds to say that he just got into a long argument with a friend about whether anyone can just walk into the local Planned Parenthood office and ask for help without parents finding out. Your son says that he is mentioning this to you because you know about such things. Much is being said and unsaid. There is the compliment about your being open to answering personal questions. You are not sure whether this is the friend's question, your son's, or the question of the entire sophomore class. You feel as if you are walking through a mine field. You think to yourself: Be frank; be informative; don't be nosy. Your son emphasizes that this is a civil rights issue—the squeal rule and teenagers. You are not convinced that this procedural issue is what is at stake. The conversation ends, and you are not sure whether you met your son's needs, either expressed or implied. Were you too nervous, prissy, full of details, or prying? Should you have explored matters further? How many of your own sexual hangups showed? You are pleased that this child, who seemed so distant these last few weeks, approached you. But did you help? What did you help?

The adolescent years are full of conversations that do not seem to get anywhere, yet are important. You wonder if you have to be board-certified as a psychiatrist to handle the flow of words properly. There are messages within messages. For example, your daughter laughingly tells you in one conversation about mindless cheerleaders, male chauvinism in the English class, and the alcohol-swilling junior high crowd that stays out late on weeknights. What might she really be saying about herself? That she is bright and perceptive, and may feel uncomfortable sometimes fitting into the social scene; that she feels pressured to do what she does not approve of, and feels that her parents do not appreciate the good thing they have in her? Do you give a speech on the dangers of alcohol and the indifference of some parents, or note what is loudly unsaid? Do you feel that you have to say something, or do you just listen?

Not only are there no neat beginnings and endings to what you do for and with children at this time, but you can almost count that they will always need your attention at inopportune times. They will regularly have crises just when you are feeling down. It is not like setting aside some special time for bedtime reading or for coaching the soccer team. Teenagers want to talk about who they are and what they stand for when they are feeling puzzled, not when you are free and feel able to cope. Big-time questions cannot be scheduled. The poster in my office reads, "Life is what happens to you while you are making other plans." That says it all. You can allocate time for the plans, but the concerns of daily living just happen to you, and you have to respond. As an adolescent, you have to figure out how you are going to respond, given your book learning to date, the values that you have been taught, and your life experience. As a parent, you facilitate this synthesis.

This aspect of being receptive to the child makes it difficult for parents who lead highly scheduled lives or who value compartmentalized, orderly existences to meet the demands of parenting at this time. They may get irritated that it takes so long to get into serious discussions, and wish that the child did not force them to show interest in preliminary sparrings before getting down to the main event of what is bothering him. Parents wish that they did not have to prove themselves, but the fact is that they do have to prove that they are available to the soon-to-be-adult child. They are not just available when it is convenient, but are available on the child's timetable. Not that a parent cannot put off a child ("I cannot talk with you now, but I want to continue this discussion when I get back"); the parent has needs, too. Individual instances of behavior do not count as much as patterns of behavior. But the parent is going to have to establish some pattern of availability that is reciprocal, rather than dictated by the parent's preferences. Parents have to prove that they are willing to take the time to draw their child out, for what is often being discussed are values that it takes a while to pursue fully.

These discussions often go something like this: The child asks the parent, "What do you think about _____?" The parent responds in detail, thinking that the child is finally interested in his point of view. When the parent comes up for air, the child is likely to say, "You say _____. Why would anyone say that?" The parent then gets annoyed that the child was not really interested in his viewpoint. This is not true, but being asked to explain his position makes the parent feel under attack.

Because he feels defensive, the parent is inclined to bluster, making his arguments seem more emotional than logical. This is pointed out by the child, who then counters with his point of view, which further convinces the parent that his own is being ignored. This is values clarification in real life. Discussion is preferred over lectures, and the child often sets the discussion up to his advantage because he is tired of his parent having the last word on every subject. (The parent who sees this coming offers fewer opinions and asks earlier, "What do you think?")

One mistake many parents make in this kind of situation is to act as if they have to respond with definitive answers when the focus is on a topic about which they continue to have an unclear point of view. This leads to rambling answers, and eventually to your child's accusation that you are being winded. It is better to say, "That is an area in which I continue to be unsure of what I believe. Do you have any thoughts on the subject?" Many of the most important questions of life do not lend themselves to quick answers. It is better to admit your confusion than to pretend to be a person given to snap judgments. The child may be relieved to find out that you are as confused as she is on the subject.

Though days were long when your children were small, there were always evenings for unwinding. You may remember many a night when you put a wide-awake child to bed in order to get some peace and quiet. The evenings were adult time for talking, reading, watching television, and making love. Bedtimes got later and later, but you still had some control over school nights. Now, that last vestige of control is disappearing. You are feeling your age and cannot keep late hours the way you once did. The child, on the other hand, thrives on nightclub hours. That is when she or he may be most communicative. You may be resigned to the fact that opportunities for conversation do not necessarily come when you are ready for them (say 8 A.M. to 9 P.M.), but will probably still be unprepared for how physically exhausting it is to be available when your child wants to talk. There is no time when you are safe from disturbance because your child has endurance, more than you have. This is a particular problem if you are a single parent with several teenagers. Just finding some special time with each child is not easy. Each child is quite different, so you hop from conversation to conversation, hoping that you will manage to keep the themes straight.

Not only is a different time configuration in operation, but spatial relationships have changed, too. In the early years, a child might be confined to a playpen, family room, or bedroom. Since you structured the day, you could call some areas your own. Now, the only space that is unquestionably yours is the one you occupy when the child is away at school. Alas, you are probably away at work at the same time. You like the child's company and want to stay in touch, so you welcome the child's enjoying home, having friends over, watching a movie on the VCR. But children of this age cannot be confined to a particular place. They get restless and rove. First, they are draped on the living room floor, next they are baking cookies in the kitchen, then they are playing Scrabble in the dining room, listening to records in a bedroom, or throwing a Frisbee outside. You cannot treat these young people as babies and tell them to stay in their place, for their place is increasingly the world. But you feel that they have taken over, and there is no place for you to be by yourself but your bedroom, where you may or may not be safe from interruptions. And you think that you are too young to have to be confined to your bedroom so early in the evening!

When the emphasis is on being responsive to the child, you may feel that means the child is always in charge, and that you have lost control. A different time or spatial configuration can leave you feeling somewhat dislocated. When the ratio of phone calls in your home is 20 for her to 1 for you, it is easy to think that you exist only to support her social life. You may yearn for a return to the time when the Fourth Commandment to love and honor parents really meant something. You imagine speaking your mind, and children accepting your word, commenting on your wisdom, and thanking you for caring. Mind you, you do not want a namby-pamby child, but you would prefer to think of yourself as active rather than responsive.

Two comments are in order. First, all authorities have reciprocal relations with their "subjects." It is inconsistent with the values of our democratic society to speak of children as subjects, although that is what they are for parents who want their children to be subject to them; but even such parents have to acknowledge the need for reciprocity. As Patricia Meyer Spacks reminds us, "Granted, children should obey parents; on the other hand, parents should avoid offending children."[4] Not offending children implies being responsive to them. Second, being responsive does mean being active, not passive. If you want to understand and influence them, then you have to listen, alert to gestures and moods; you have to comment appropriately. That does not mean that you are passive about either your feelings or beliefs. You do not just reflect back to children what they have said, but share your views. If the child feels misunderstood, for example, part of the discussion may involve admitting that you sometimes feel misunderstood by her or him.

Being responsive means that you do not react to what is said with the first thought that comes into your head. For example, your child says, "I hate your friends; they're so boring," and you retort, "How dare you say that about my friends? Yours are the ones who are really stupid." Instead, you assume that the words have been said to grab your attention and respond with that old standard, "Why do you say that?" inviting your child to expand her ideas. While she is talking, you are considering what she really means: Does she feel tongue-tied with adults? Are you spending too much time with your friends and not enough time with her? Are your friends treating her like a little girl? Do you expect her to be seen and not heard when your friends are around? The point is not to treat remarks as accusations and become defensive, but to regard them as a dramatic (even melodramatic) way of seeing whether you will take her seriously and pursue the matter. As the conversation progresses, you may both wind up discussing how you might get along better with each other's friends.

It is not easy to have such conversations of mutual exploration. In theory, they sound reasonable; in practice, issues surface when you feel least eager to get into a philosophical discussion. Pat answers are so much quicker! After a hard day of work, you feel more like watching television with a cold drink in hand than discussing issues that you have spent years trying not to think about too much (e.g., God, love, friendship, evil in the world, the meaning of life). But your child needs you to extend yourself so she can think out loud with you by her side, and these conversations can be stimulating. What is more, she will take you more seriously if you take her seriously.

The truth is that most of us parents want our children to be "ours" forever. We are not ready for a truly mutual relationship. Our notion of mutuality is to want to define those areas in which reciprocal relations can exist. We are used to giving children second-order choices, after we have winnowed down the possibilities. "Do you want to wear the red, blue, or white dress?" as a choice makes wearing a dress non-negotiable. Eda J. LeShan wisely entitled one chapter in her book, *How to Survive Parenthood:* "We All Wanted *Babies*—but Did Any of Us Want Children?"[5] And if the transition from babies to children is not easy, then the transition from children to adults is a hundred times more dificult. As they become increasingly competent, children regularly make us feel useless. They also remind us that we may not be as grownup as we claim to be. LeShan entitled another chapter, "If You Are a Parent It Helps If You Are Grown-Up," and urged parents to confront their basic attitudes towards growth: "Are we really and genuinely for it; do we accept it; and can we adapt to it?"[6]

The second decade of parenthood is a time when you have to recognize fully that children have wills of their own, and are entitled to their viewpoints and to consideration. Changes in the child's physical appearance force parents to face the need for new ways of relating. It is no longer reasonable, if it ever was, for the child to be excluded from decisions that affect her or him, since the countdown is under way for the child's launching as a self-sufficient member of society. If you are the type who has benign-dictator leanings, you are used to informing after the fact. You are ill-prepared for the child's refusal to remain passive and dependent. You are not prepared for "talking back" because you define it as disrespectful rather than necessary.

Talking back is the way young people grow up and achieve their own sense of identity. They challenge the old terms of the parent-child relationship; in articulating their views, they gain a better understanding of their own positions. Because parents are inclined to want their family to be safe, soothing haven from outside stresses, they are likely to view any conflict in negative terms. To them, conflict means enmity rather than innovation. If talking back can be regarded as disruptive for a purpose, then it can be seen as potentially creative. The problem is that most parents are initially inclined to be defensive; they are more likely to see challenges to the old order as criticisms of their ability than as proof that they have successfully raised a thinker. If, however, conflict can be understood as having constructive consequences, the parents will be more likely to respond to a challenge with "That is a really good point, but did you consider _____?" This kind of response is part of a healthy system of checks and balances between the generations.

If parents are inclined not to recognize the positive aspects of conflict, their children are not inclined to recognize the positive aspects of parents' asking for proof of their responsibility when new freedoms are demanded. When parents set limits, the child is forced to argue that he can be adequate to the task at hand. In convincing them, he convinces himself that he can do what he needs to do. This does not mean that parents should raise bogus barriers to slow the child down, but their hesitancies do serve the purpose of slowing the scramble for independence to a manageable, less scary pace.

These are the years when parents have to help their children become self-sufficient, and that implies being sympathetic to all that the child is experiencing. For all the caring that most parents feel, they often do not pause to look at the child's world with sympathy. The weekday hours are highly structured; children usually do not have a minute to call their own from about 6:30 A.M. to 3:30 P.M. (lengthy commutes to and from school can extend this time much further). Work follows them home; by the time they are in the junior high years, homework can range from one to four hours per day. Add to that schedule piano lessons, track, rehearsals for the school play, selling raffle tickets, student council meetings, chores, religious education, etc., and you have a full week. Despite recent complaints about the quality of education, young people exist in a world of tough standards; some of them work their best and have only a C – to show for their effort. The school atmosphere may be repressive; it often is an environment more aimed at controlling behavior than educating the mind. Next, take account of the worries that concern just about every teenager: Am I attractive? Is there life after high school? Finally, most young people are concerned to some extent about money, either working part-time or figuring out how they can stretch their resources to get what they want. This is the profile of individuals entitled to their viewpoints and to consideration. Bear in mind that this sanitized profile completely ignored the special concerns that make life even more difficult for hundreds of thousands of adolescents: poverty, chronic health problems (e.g., allergies, diabetes, epilepsy, leukemia), alcoholic parents, rough neighborhoods, drug traffic, etc.

Parenting at this age is largely responsive, has no neat beginnings and endings, and acknowledges the will of the child. It is also likely to make you feel incompetent regularly. In the early years, the child needed to learn what most of us know— how to walk, talk, avoid soggy pants, tell time, count change, read, and write. With each successive year, the frustrations experienced by the child become more complicated. As a parent, you try to be of help, but there are more and more areas in which you cannot be of direct help. The child needs tutoring with trigonometry and your schooling did not go beyond algebra. The child is working on a mechanical hand for a science fair, and the only thought you have is that your hands have some arthritis. The child has problems moving a paragraph on the computer, and you are a person who still has not gotten used to electric typewriters, much less word processing. The child asks your advice about a writing assignment, incorporates your suggestions, and gets a C. You feel as if you are flunking out as a parent; you should have been able to do better than that.

No amount of logical talk about how ridiculous it is to infer from three or four helpless moments that you are totally inept can eliminate those waves of insecurity. You assumed parenthood convinced that you would be more or less adequate to the tasks to come. You may never have equated parenthood with mathematical ability, but you can still feel incompetent when those areas in which you cannot help your child start to accumulate.

The answer, of course, is to reframe parenthood so that it no longer means you provide solutions, but help the child find resources so she or he can resolve a problem. This makes sense, but feelings are not always sensible. You, the parent, may be overwhelmed by your worthlessness, which is magnified because you are going through the painful stocktaking of middle age. It does not help when your daughter teases you, "Mom, what are you good for?" after you have not been able to do something. No real offense is meant. The child is just pleased to announce that the person who once seemed larger than life is not perfect; that gives her hope. She sees you as having done well even though you are not without faults, so maybe she can succeed, too. You, on the other hand, may be going through one of your normal paranoid moments and take umbrage, because you still retain the dated notion that you have to be all things to her.

If this is the case, you will not be ready for other adults becoming important in your child's life. Adolescence is a time when children develop special relationships with teachers, coaches, neighbors, youth leaders, aunts, and uncles. Young people are delighted when they find adults, other than their parents, who enjoy them and take them seriously. But parents may not be prepared for dinnertime conversations about how wonderful Mrs. X and Mr. Y are. The parent thinks, I do more for this child than Mrs. X and Mr. Y ever will, and does that get noticed? It is particularly annoying when you say something and get ignored, but someone else says the very same thing and it is treated as gospel! You feel set aside and undervalued. You are a bit like the child who is wondering if he will still be loved when a new brother appears on the scene. These feelings normally happen, especially if you are a single parent used to being *the* adult in your child's life. You will be less sorry for yourself if you realize both that you are responsible for the child's being ready to branch out and that these important others are ways of meeting children's needs in areas where your own competence is limited. Besides, your child is bound to think more highly of you when the letting go is over, and he looks at you with the perspective that is not possible at close range!

Parents should not be ashamed when they feel incompetent. Children need you to admit that you have inept moments; this means that they do not have to worry about being perfect in order to be any good. Do not flaunt your inadequacies so you become an object of pity. Just recognize that your limitations can be put to use. Young people need their parents to be optimistic about their futures, and one way you can be optimistic is to share with your child those areas where she or he is ahead of you: You have a way of making people feel good about themselves that it took me thirty years to learn, and not as well. . . . When I was your age, I was not as poised as you are. . . . You seem to find easy those things that I have always found difficult. . . . You are better than I am when it comes to math. . . . I am a klutz; I so admire your ability to work with your hands.

Most of us hesitate to display our weaknesses, thinking that we will be devalued, but we are often valued more for being honest about ourselves. For example, singer Billy Joel is admired even more by teenagers for admitting that he came close to suicide when he was twenty and checked into a hospital for help. When you hide your failures, much of your energy is consumed in keeping up appearances, and you often look pompous. When you admit your struggles, you teach the important lesson of how to live with mistakes.

It used to be easier to improve on your parents' lives. Just by graduating from high school I was able to accomplish something my parents admired. By our late twenties, my husband and I owned a home; my parents did not have one of their own until they were fifty-eight. Now the world has changed, and children who have grown up with middle-class expectations do not know if they can even maintain the lifestyle to which they have become accustomed, much less surpass it. One gift that parents can give their children is to stop feeling guilty about their own inadequacies and tell their children that they will be able to accomplish something admirably that the older generation found difficult. Such positive reinforcement does not give children a "big head," but lets them know that you are excited about their possibilities. In a world full of headlines about shortages, inflation, limited resources, nuclear fallout, and the fast track, children need the sense that they are ahead in some way. This becomes particularly important if the child is neither brilliant, gorgeous, nor headed for the Olympics, but has qualities that are not praised enough in school, for example, perception, a pleasant disposition, attention to detail, a sense of humor, optimism in the face of troubles, starch in her backbone.

Parenting during these years may seem like a kamikaze mission. You are being asked to be available to your children in a way that many trained professionals find difficult, by listening to both spoken and unspoken words. You will be discussing issues that have no pat answers. When problems surface, you will often feel ill-prepared to handle them. Your child is bound to feel some ambivalence about you: What self-respecting adolescent wants to be seen as tied to apron strings? You are likely to feel angry because you do not remember your own parents being available to you at this age the way you try to be with your child, and yet there is no appreciation. And, what is more, it is even difficult to describe what you do. If someone asked you what you do these days as a parent, you would feel tongue-tied to answer the question.

The central dilemma of parenting during these years is that you have to transfer power over to your child during a time when you remain constantly reminded that you are ultimately responsible for anything that may go wrong. If you do not gradually empower the child to make her own decisions, she will not have learned how to do so when she reaches her majority. It is irresponsible to prevent her from growing up, but you want to postpone it until she is more responsible. But she will never act more responsibly until she is expected to be responsible. This is not an impossible position to be in, but it may feel impossible on a day-to-day basis. The key is to link increments in power with proof of increased responsibility. The child takes on something new, you evaluate how it was handled, and then you pull back or push forward accordingly: Two steps ahead . . . one step back . . . three steps ahead . . . one step back. . . . All the stops and starts are part of the moves of these years.

Though the tasks of the second decade of parenthood are not easy, the pleasures of this period of parenting are very special. There is the pleasure of having another grownup in the house for good conversation. There is the joy of seeing the child nicknamed Poky because she always dawdled, arranging for a summer job, and responsibly meeting workplace expectations. You no longer have to do everything for the child; the child can do so much for you—drive a younger brother to school, pick up a prescription at the drugstore, look up a bus schedule. You can weave the subject matter of a child's term paper into your own work: The philosophy professor compares the priest-penitent relationship (the daughter's research) to the doctor-patient relationship in her class on biomedical ethics; the farmer learns something new about plant genetics from his daughter's 4H project; the reporter thinks the subject matter of her child's paper—teenage suicide—would make a fine feature story; the store owner gets marketing ideas from listening to his son talk about why he did not buy something. The child uses pink mousse for her hair, and you decide that your hair could profit from added body and auburn highlights. When you are hosting a party, your sons provide you with records and tapes that expand your taste beyond Nat "King" Cole and Kenny Rogers.

Not all parents will find these years equally pleasurable. There is some evidence that less well-educated women prefer the early years of child development, whereas better-educated mothers prefer late adolescence. It may be that the competency issues of this period are more threatening if you are less educated:

> Education matters far less in relations between parents and the very young child, since child rearing at this stage involves teaching basic language and motor skills at which parents of all levels of sophistication may be quite competent. But educated parents may seek to order life's affairs in a predictable manner that early child rearing is bound to upset, so they may find early child rearing upsetting to their daily routines and life styles. Once children reach adolescence, an educated parent may have more in common with the high school or college age child than less well-educated parents have.[7]

Expense may be another factor. Better-educated parents, with higher status jobs and greater income, are more able to handle the financial burdens of these years than their less affluent counterparts. Whether both parents have an employment history may be yet another factor. If both parents have worked for years outside the home, they may have encouraged independence all along, so their child's self-determination may please more than distress them.

But the background of the parents need not make a decisive difference in enjoyment of these years. Attitude, which you can control because it is constructed out of your basic beliefs, is the key. It is important that parents' beliefs about this period include certain mind-sets—for example, that much teenage rebellion makes developmental sense; that adolescence is not a time for parental complacency; that young people are interesting and stimulating. The negative side to these years is often associated with the problems of being overstimulated. Rapier-sharp wit can cut; figuring out both the spoken and unspoken messages can be exhausting. On the positive side, however, you have a life of zest, spirit, ginger, and drive. It can be just the tonic for middle-aged torpor. Your ideas are challenged, and that keeps you on your toes and your brain cells making connections. You confront new ideas, and that can have a bracing effect. Your child's interests can stretch you in directions that give you added possibilities. It helps to see the experience as energizing, not enervating.

· 5 ·

SAVING YOUR
CHILD FROM
MAKING MISTAKES

When their children are teenagers, the principal objective of many parents is to save their children from making mistakes. The teenage years have such a reputation for TROUBLE that safekeeping becomes a parental obsession. Anytime the teen years are discussed, there is a tendency to focus on the trouble young people get into, even though the overwhelming majority of adolescents never get into serious trouble. Trouble tends to be equated with a lack of parental control—parents "let" their children get into trouble, so setting limits is seen as the answer to most problems. It is no wonder that a social analysis of parenting at adolescence frequently centers on parents as exercisers of social control.[1] Parenting during these years is identified with screening, monitoring, warning, reminding, cautioning, admonishing, scolding, and threatening. Parents do not want their children to get hurt, either physically or psychologically. That seems a worthy priority. Who could argue with that? The children, that is who. They wonder, Whose life is it anyway?

It is normal to have savior tendencies when you feel responsible. When the child is young, parents want to prevent skinned knees, spills, breaks, and temper tantrums. As the child grows older, they want to prevent her or him from going into a car with strangers, poor reading habits, loneliness, and apathy. By the teen years, most parents feel compelled to do everything they can to prevent drunk driving, adolescent pregnancy, doped brains, and tangles with the law. Over the years, they move from worrying about things that they can more or less control to matters that often seem beyond their control. They move from worrying about private foibles to being concerned about behavior in the public arena. Parents at this point often redouble their savior efforts because they are worried about the child's making big-time mistakes that have dire consequences for others. This happens just when children want some room to experiment.

One has to feel sorry for the parents' dilemma: They are legally responsible for what the child does until the age of eighteen, but they cannot keep telling the child what to do because they want the child to reach that age having learned how to assume personal responsibility. The only way to develop into a trustworthy person is to handle graded responsibilities. The problem is you never can be sure whether you are expecting too much or too little, for sometimes the child acts fifteen going on thirty-nine and other times the same child is fifteen sliding back to six. There are no set rules, but there are daily questions: When do you give up baby-sitters and leave the child home alone past midnight? Do you allow your son to get one ear pierced when you know that some adults will look askance and be prejudiced against him? May your daughter decide to stop attending church services? Should your seventeen-year-old drive a carload of friends sixty miles to a band contest? None of these questions lends itself to pat answers; they all involve discussing the matter with the child and assessing her or his perceptions. Parents worry that they will be in the wrong if things do not go right, but they are more likely to have to deal with problems if decisions are not shared with the child.

The mistake parents make is to think that such questions are ones that should be answered yes or no. For example, you leave children at home past midnight only when they have had previous positive experiences with being alone—first during the day, then later and later into the evening—with numbers to call in case of emergencies. And if there are several children, you have to talk over matters with each child in order to assess whether past experiences have been generally positive, because needs vary by individual. You do not automatically say, "No, you cannot have your ear pierced," or "No, you cannot stop attending church," until you find out what is behind the questions: Does your son want to look like a buccaneer for his girlfriend? Does he realize that some potential employers or teachers may decide that he is wild and untrustworthy if he looks that way? Does your daughter have misgivings about the worth of religion that might be explored? Would she prefer to attend another church that has an active youth group? Is she mainly pushing for the right to sit with friends at the service and not with her parents? The child who asks about driving a carload of friends may want you to say "No" so that she has an excuse to get out of being responsible for the safety of peers whom she cannot control, but that, too, should not be resolved on face value.

It is never easy for parents to agree on the exact approach to take with their children, so tensions between mother and father are especially likely to mount during these years. The father thinks it is too soon for the daughter to wear makeup; the mother sees nothing wrong in the daughter's experimenting with eye shadow and lip gloss in order to learn how to use them artfully. The father sees no harm in the son's having regular use of the family car; the mother regards that practice as an invitation to trouble. The mother regards the child's constant comments about being bored as evidence of restless intelligence; the father looks at the same behavior and interprets it as proof of a shallow personality. The child writes her mother and stepfather a note saying that she hates them: The stepfather concludes that the child is hateful; the mother sees herself as having been so successful that her daughter can communicate strong feelings directly. One parent wants a strict curfew in order to avoid trouble; the other urges flexibility in order to prevent rebellion. Observing the same behavior, there is some evidence that mothers are more likely than fathers to perceive the child as somewhat troubled, so a basic difference in the assumptions made by parents may exist at the start of any discussion.[2] For example, the mother looks at her son's feistiness and sees insecurity, whereas the father sees meanness.

There is also some tendency for parents to act differently, depending on the sex of the child. Parents may be predisposed to protect daughters, yet push sons to be adventuresome. This mind-set does not go over well with the daughter who adamantly refuses to be held back by female stereotypes. The daughter rebels and the parents may overreact simply because any rebellion is regarded as excessive, since it is not an accepted part of traditional femininity. There seems to be a cross-gender effect operating, too; parents may be inclined to be more supportive of the child of the other sex. For example, mothers with sons and fathers with daughters seem to be less negative verbally than mothers with daughters and fathers with sons.[3] Parents may be more demanding of the child of the same sex because they know what they went through and managed. The father may be worried about his daughter's depression, while the mother is thinking, It's not that bad compared to what I went through when I was her age; she will eventually pull herself together.

Divorced couples have a particularly difficult time at this

point. Tempers flare because there are so many judgment calls and opportunities for disagreement. The custodial parent may see that the child needs some growing room now that she is in high school, whereas the parent without day-to-day contact may argue for stricter discipline as the answer to all problems because that has worked in the past. One parent may focus on the child's not being smothered; the other may think the child needs structure. If the parents have themselves remarried, the opinions of a stepmother and stepfather can add to the strains.

If the parents realize that no one viewpoint is likely to be totally correct, they may see an advantage to different perspectives. Different viewpoints can play off each other. Ideally, sessions of point-counterpoint lead to richer solutions: The bias one person has is counteracted by the bias of the other, leading to a third (and better) conclusion. When a mother believes, This child needs our support, and the father thinks, This child is wrapping his mother around his little finger, the chances are that together they are providing the child with some combination of sympathy and prodding that is meeting the needs of different pieces of his situation. That is, they are meeting his needs so long as they focus on him, and not on proving each other wrong. Alas, they may take the easy way out and fight with each other in order to avoid dealing with a son who remains something of an enigma to both of them.

One has to feel sorry for children, too. They are told to act mature, but may not be trusted to make any decisions that matter to them. Their parents may ask their opinions, then voice their own before the child is finished talking. As one child noted, "They want you to have your say, but what they are for is all that is permitted to be said." Children do not want to hurt these beloved individuals, to whom so much is owed, but parents act crazy at times, as if every push the child makes to be independent were a nail in their parents' coffins.

Parents want their children to be responsible, but often only on the parents' terms. In some instances, children wish parents would stop haranguing them about taking too many chances, because knee-jerk naysaying on the part of parents often has the contrary effect of making children determined to take chances, some of which are even against the children's better judgment. The child wishes her parents would lighten up and just appreciate her; they seem to be so caught up with their response to her that they lose sight of what she is asking. The child is full of questions: Do they trust me? If so, why are they constantly checking up on me? Why do they tend to talk to me as if I were younger than I am? Can I trust my parents not to read my mail or my diary, and not to rummage through my drawers? Do they really try to see my side? Do they realize how responsible I am compared with other teenagers? Why am I always the person who is expected to give in if there is a disagreement?

Although there are no ironclad rules for setting limits without killing experimentation, some guidelines can be applied: (a) Teenagers should have plenty of opportunities to make truly independent choices in both trivial and important matters; (b) responsibilities and privileges should be balanced; (c) working out privileges and responsibilities is a cooperative venture; (d) expectations should be reviewed regularly because the children's situation is constantly changing; (e) parents should act consistently in implementing decisions reached.

Lois and Joel Davitz, wife and husband psychologists, have this advice to offer about important decisions: "When your adolescent faces important, complicated decisions with potentially serious, long-term consequences, be sure you make clear the realistic limits within which any decision must be made."[4] Articulate the limits ahead of time, so it will not look as if the child can decide anything. But once limits are set, the child should have responsibility for making thoughtful decisions within those limits. Parents provide information, opinions, and advice, but their role, except for boundary issues, is as a major consultant, not as the principal decision-maker on day-to-day issues.

What does it mean for the parent to specify clear-cut limits? In one household, it means parents make most decisions that have to do with long-term health and safety, whereas other decisions are usually left up to the teenagers as long as they obey rules and laws, stay out of serious trouble, and are where they belong when they belong there. This is a far from precise statement of limits, for parents and children may hold very different opinions about where they belong and when they belong there. But in this family, young people are generally free to make their own decisions about hair and dress, friends, school courses, religious preference, the way they keep their room, choice of doctor and dentist, extracurricular activities, and when to do their homework. That provides children with considerable latitude. Obviously, families will vary in their description of the limits within which teenagers are expected to operate, but the task for all families is to be clear about what they are. There have to be limits, but they should not be drawn so tightly as to preclude genuine decision-making on the part of the child.

Even those parents who are only comfortable drawing rather tight limits should keep in mind that their children should decide how these expectations are to be realized. If the assumption is that the child attends church, then he should be able to decide whether he attends the morning or evening service and where he sits in church. If the child is responsible for weekly cleaning, then she should be able to decide how she is going to get the job done. If the child is expected to go to the family dentist, then he should be able to schedule appointments at his convenience.

Parents are not likely to think much about setting limits until pressed by the child. The child pushes and the parents react. They feel nettled by request after request, and wish the child would just leave them alone. The tendency is to want to exert strict controls, so the pushing will not escalate. But strict controls lead to more arguments about what is fair. This is the time to set general limits, so the child can have the experience of self-determination within some boundaries. Limits are best set by starting off asking the child, "What do you think is reasonable?" Many times children actually will argue for less than you think they want.

Whatever limits are set, it also helps to admit from the start that there are bound to be exceptions to most rules. For example, curfews can be modified on special occasions. If something unexpected happens, the child should be instructed to call home and say she will be late, without incurring any penalty. As the child gets older, it helps if parents remember when setting limits that it will be only a short time before they will have no say. If you will not know what the child is doing next year when he is in the army, it makes sense to allow a certain latitude in the here and now, so all members of the family can get ready for the new ways of relating to come.

Setting guidelines for handling graded responsibilities may be less important than the psychology of the situation. Most parents have some sense that you make decisions in keeping with the child's capabilities, and talk over what seems reasonable in a particular situation. What is less clear is why parents do not act that way even when they believe that they should do so. There obviously are strong feelings and some unreasonable thoughts that influence interactions. How does the parent feel about not being the decision-maker but only a valued consultant? Angry or confused, because there is some sense of having been replaced? How much is the parent's behavior a consequence of not being ready for the child to move in new directions? Most parents are unprepared for children to make decisions as early as they push to do so. How much is the parent's protectiveness the result of caring and how much are the cautionary tales a way of scaring the child into submission? If trial and error is important in learning how to behave properly, then why do parents limit trial and error on the grounds of avoiding mistakes? Is it because they fundamentally believe either that experimentation is wrong or that every trial-and-error sequence has to be followed by trial and success?

Parents have to confront their secret expectations. Do they have unarticulated rules of thumb that do not permit many mistakes? For example, that every attempt to do something new can be followed by only one mistake or two at the most, and never by three or more. Just confronting these secret expectations can be the jolt you need to appreciate how silly and unreasonable they are. In some areas, it takes a long time to get things right. Developing a sense of style takes months, even years, of experimentation with hair, makeup, and clothes. You should not sigh in disgust when your son cannot seem to learn how to parallel park; it takes considerable practice for some people to develop that spatial ability.

Parents' behavior can be better understood if it is examined with regard to the meaning attached to "mistakes." Regardless of how liberal parents sometimes sound, most of them have difficulty with the notion that their child will make mistakes. Parents grant the right to make mistakes to others, but may still cling to the notion, It will be different with my child. There is the hope that the parent will either do something or not do something, so as to limit the mistakes her/his child will make. The fact that the child has made mistakes, which you previously thought could be avoided, at the age of three or seven or ten does not preclude parents from hoping that it will be different at twelve or fifteen and eighteen. They keep hoping that they will finally get parenting right and, with it, achieve the perfect child!

Why do parents cling to this naïve hope? The child is the

parents' report card. If their children do well, parents know they have done well. If their children make mistakes, parents feel as if the mistake is theirs. This is faulty logic, but society continues to reinforce such connections every time a parent is complimented for being responsible for a child's achievements or castigated for a child's bungling. Parents who are in the helping professions may have a particular problem with handling mistakes, because the child's problems can also make them look or feel like professional failures.

There is, of course, some relationship between parents' and child's behavior, but the bizarre linear thinking that prevails just makes parents overly sensitive about mistakes and, consequently, insensitive about relating to the child who has made a mistake. Parents are overly sensitive because they take every miscalculation on the part of the child personally: "He did that to me." They are insensitive in dealing with the child because they are more absorbed with their response to the situation rather than with the child's response to his mistake.

This mind-set is unreceptive to the notion that each time you misjudge you may learn how to make a better judgment the next time around. You learn from your mistakes if you have time to reflect on what you did wrong and how that might be avoided in the future. Parents who think in terms of "your mistake is my mistake" are not likely to facilitate this learning. Such parents may admit the child's right to make mistakes, but they often get so concerned that it not happen again (that would really be a MISTAKE), that they are not truly available for rehashing the matter in a way that would be helpful to the child. The negative overlay that is part of the parent's response makes interacting with the parent uncomfortable for the child, just when the child needs an environment conducive to dealing with difficult matters.

Parents are used to making mistakes; they have had a lifetime of experience. Then why do they shy away from the prospect of their children being like them? It may be that they still think their mistakes could have been avoided, if they had only had different parents. To the extent that they tried their very best, correcting what was lacking in their own childhoods, they may be ill-prepared for the child's limitations. They think, After all that I have done, how could you do this? Instead of realizing that mistakes are part of the human experience, they may conclude that "this child is hopeless," and give up. The assumption is that if this child had been redeemable, then the parents' noble intentions would have carried the day.

Another reason parents do not accord their child the same right to make mistakes which they have granted themselves, is that many of their mistakes have achieved the status of imperfections or personality idiosyncrasies. They see that nothing disastrous happened as a consequence of the jams they got into twenty years ago. Sure, parents are not proud of some moments, but they feel that they have turned out more or less okay. The mother may remember the date with a man who turned out to be strange, but she is not sure that her daughter would know enough to get out of the same difficult situation by pretending to be sick the way she did. The father may remember when he spent a weekend lost to reefers or alcohol, but he is not sure that his son would know, the way he now does, that too many lost weekends just make you a loser. Parents cannot be sure that their teenagers' experimentation will just become interesting stories two decades later the way theirs have. Especially if they had some narrow escapes, parents may not want their own children to have any close calls.

Another reason parents have problems with mistakes is that they do not expect trouble, particularly if they have done everything they can to avoid it. They deny that grief, disappointment, and problems are as much a part of life experience as joy, accomplishment, and pleasure. Our contraceptive society, with its emphasis on control, may also have inadvertently given us the message that mistakes can be avoided, which leaves us unprepared for the human condition.

You may be conscientious about providing information for all occasions. You may try to do everything you can to make sure the child is allowed space, but not so much that she or he will flounder. You may encourage the child to study the topic from all angles before making a decision. You may stress the importance of listing your options in every situation. You may remind the child that going along with the crowd may have negative consequences that no crowd can help you shoulder. But all of these preparations, important as they are, are no substitute for considering whether you are up to handling mistakes so they can be a growth experience.

There is not much challenge in being caring and gracious when things go well; the test is how you behave when things do not go well. Children are afraid that if they make mistakes their parents will say, "I told you so, but you never listen," and withdraw into cold smugness. Or they worry, "If my parents ever knew that, it would kill them." Parents, too, are afraid that they will not be able to handle major problems. Often parents are so concerned about what might happen that they worry loudly (and disproportionately) over small matters. It is magical thinking: If you put in enough worry time, then nothing truly horrendous will happen. But this kind of behavior may only have the effect of convincing your child that you cannot take real life. You worry so much when nothing much is the matter, how will you handle something really going wrong?

One of the major tasks of the adolescent years is to prove both to your child and to yourself that you can take real life and so can she. The child does not always have to come to you with honor-roll grades, achievements, and funny stories for you to care. You are there for the difficult moments, too. It helps to imagine some worst-case scenarios and what might be the preferred response: Would you help a son with venereal disease? (This child needs medical attention, information, and support to act responsibly with his partner[s].) Could you cope if your child were to blame for an automobile accident in which one of the passengers was seriously hurt? (Take it a day at a time; don't lose this child as well as the other one.) What would you do if your child were suspended from school for having drugs? (Wonder what clues along the way were missed, and what help is available for such a problem.) What would you do if your daughter got into a fight and broke someone else's nose, and that child's parents sued? (Discover what happened, and get a good lawyer.) What would you do if you found out that your daughter was pregnant? (Find out how she feels about the situation before shouting out your opinions.)

No one instinctively handles such situations smoothly. You may want to curse the gods for the plague visited upon your house, then curse your child for being a plague. But could you handle the situation—that is, not be so paralyzed by your emotions that at least part of you was available to listen to how the child felt and to support the child in living with the consequences? All of these things can happen without the child's being incorrigible. How you handle them could make the difference between children learning an enormous amount from the experience and children figuring that if you are going to treat them as foul they will really make a big stink.

A problem, no matter how major, should never wipe out past accomplishments or eliminate the possibility of future successes. Parents have to keep that in mind. It helps, I think, to remember that in some very public failures—Chappaquiddick and Watergate, for example—the issue became less the problems themselves than how they were handled. Accidents and stupidities happen, but there are better and worse ways of responding to them. You try to avoid problems, but when they happen, you focus on doing the best with a bad situation, rather than wishing you could turn the clock back. Senator Edward Kennedy and former President Richard Nixon have also both demonstrated that you can move beyond being mired in your personal failures and go on to contribute to the public good (one through a commitment to health and welfare legislation; the other through his writings). If these men can be rehabilitated in the public eye, then your prodigal child can be restored to your family.

You hope your child will never get into serious trouble, but crises happen. The advantage to imagining your own worst-case scenario is that, hopefully, you can see that you could live through the event and still function. Recognizing that you are resilient can then affect how you handle more mundane affairs. The key to all crises is not to overreact, not to let all your pent-up frustrations spill over in a stream of invectives aimed at the child. It is easy to get caught up with "you did this to me" thinking, when the child is the one who has the problem.

If you can imagine that you could handle a particularly difficult situation by being available to the child, then you may be better able to manage lesser offenses without a tirade. As one mother said,

> My fourteen-year-old son surprised me by cleaning out the fireplace, but unthinkingly left the bag of ashes, with some burning embers, on the rug. A portion of the forty-year-old rug was scorched by the time we smelled the trouble. If I had not been at home, our Victorian house could have gone up in smoke. I was fit to be tied, until I saw how utterly devastated my son was; that made me stop fuming. Nothing really bad had happened, but I learned from that incident that my son is more important than any house. Having confronted something awful in my head, I am not bothered as much by small things like broken dishes or ink on the upholstery.

The message you convey when you can handle a child's mistakes is that the child can handle her or his mistakes, too. If you treat the problem as beyond help, then the child is paralyzed and feels beyond redemption. Children should not have to be absolutely perfect in order to be supported and found lovable. Oddly enough, it is especially important that parents of successful children appreciate this. Parents with A+ children may be unprepared for handling even relatively minor problems, because they have had no previous experience. The first time something major goes wrong, they may fulminate in order to "nip the problem in the bud," leaving their chilren with distorted impressions of themselves. When you have grown up expected to be blameless, you may have self-esteem too brittle to handle much failure. In certain situations, the "perfect" child may start to become obsessed with suicidal thoughts because mistakes have assumed a larger-than-life quality. This may be precipitated by parents' having emphasized in the months and years before the mistake that their child was not the type to make a major blunder. This thinking can leave the child convinced that the parents will not be able to handle anything approaching a major blunder, and neither can he. Mistakes should never seem larger than life.

Most children are very sorry for their mistakes. They appreciate parents who put things into perspective—"Don't worry about breaking that; may that be your biggest problem in life." It helps if you can acknowledge that this infraction is unusual for them when it is out of character—"I know that you are not usually careless, that is all the more reason for not getting overly excited about this." Standing by your child without exploding can be the turning point in a relationship. One father seemed to have argument after argument with his son. The son went out one evening and wrapped the family car around a telephone pole. He was convinced that this would be the final rupture and his father would disown him. Instead, his father helped him deal with the insurance company and went with him to his court hearing. The father was angry with the child, but his feelings did not paralyze him into inaction. Five years later, the child remembers that time with some fondness, for it was the beginning of a new level of intimacy between them— and also the beginning of the son's becoming appreciably more responsible.

Standing by children does not mean that children escape the consequences of their behavior. It means you support them as they deal with the consequences of their behavior. Some parents withdraw support in the face of trouble because they "want the child to have the book thrown at him, so he'll never do it again." This is being vindictive rather than instructive. Parents who "fix" speeding tickets do not help children learn to be more responsible, but parents who withdraw all support can make their children feel victimized instead of responsible. There is a point beyond which punishment can be too demeaning, out of proportion to the offense, and the perpetrator becomes calloused rather than repentant.

How the child handles mistakes is related to whether parents are perceived as people to whom a person can tell problems. Parents who automatically roll their eyes heavenwards or sigh loudly when a child misjudges do not inspire confidences. The first words said should not be, "It's all your fault. . . ." Nor does it help to have the opposite happen, to be told that it is everyone else's fault—"Your friends are nothing but jerks and got you into trouble." Alas, parents sometimes tend to be more open and sympathetic to the problems of everyone else but their children. This should not be too surprising because distance does make possible a better sense of perspective. Granted that this is true, it may help to ask, "How would I feel if this had happened to someone else?" in order to gain some understanding closer to home. Because parents have some predisposition to make sure that the child does not falter again, they may be bent on transforming a bad situation into one of life's lessons, with a vengeance. That inclination makes them preachy, less available to "be" for the child.

Parents sometimes have the attitude that they exist to point out to children the evil of their ways—or so it seems to the children. Their chant goes on: "Don't do . . . Watch out . . . Stop it . . . No. . . ." They act as if they have been empowered to eliminate mistakes for all eternity. But do parents notice when the child heeds these words? Parents are much more likely to notice problems than to spotlight improvement. "Trying hard" and "being good" are too often dismissed as behavior that is expected and, therefore, ignored. The parent thinks, Why should I have to praise her for acting well? No one pats me on the shoulder for acting well. Parents have a point: They are not praised much when they do well (it is taken for granted), but they are certainly faulted when things go wrong (they should know better). This wears them down, and makes them more likely to focus on eliminating the negative and less likely to accentuate the positive.

The focus on the negative is also part of being middle-aged. To the extent that parents are asking of their lives, "Is that all there is?" they may weave their children's mistakes into the faultfinding pattern of this period. This leaves them attending to only a portion of their children's behavior. The children develop the notion that acting well does not get noticed; positive behaviors are discounted. The result can be the exact opposite of what is intended. One of the most dispiriting things that can happen is for your efforts to be dismissed as just what is expected. This places the person with the high expectations, rather than the person who performed well, in a complimentary light. And if you do not think that what you do counts, you become more likely to make mistakes.

Sometimes parents think that accentuating the positive just gives children big heads. What they forget is that focusing on the negative gives you no head, meaning a sense of yourself as a competent person. To the extent that parents are angry because no one pats them on the shoulder, they should make their feelings known rather than just pass on the old behavior to the next generation. This involves reminding children that they cannot just tell you when you have failed as a parent (a subject dear to the hearts of most teenagers), but have to notice when you have made a special effort. Otherwise, you will be too dispirited to notice when they have made a special effort.

How the child handles mistakes is also related to how parents treat their mistakes. And they do make mistakes, many of them, in parenting their children! The old notion was that parents, particularly fathers, should never admit to making mistakes lest authority be lost. The assumption was that you lose authority once those you direct see that you make mistakes: Who wants to be instructed by someone who does not know what he is doing? The flaw in this line of reasoning is that it is impossible never to make a mistake. If you pretend to be blameless, you look worse than you do when you admit to being less than perfect. An admission of error allows all concerned to proceed with the business at hand, otherwise authority figures are putting all their energies into keeping up appearances, and those subject to such authority are putting all their energies into proving that appearances are deceiving.

Seeing parents live with their mistakes, on the other hand, reminds children that they can live with their mistakes. Transgressions and embarrassing incidents can be overcome, if not always easily. Role models are important, especially if the behavior under scrutiny is awkward, delicate, and not easily tackled. Handling mistakes can be a formidable lesson in bravery.

Apologies are the keystone in handling mistakes. They serve an important function in acting responsibly:

From a societal perspective, apologies are social conventions that perform a variety of important functions, including serving as recognition that rules have been broken, reaffirming the value of the rules, and controlling and regulating social conduct by acknowledging the existence of interpersonal obligations. From the perspective of the actor who appears responsible for the incident, apologies also function as remedial behaviors that attempt to minimize the negative repercussions of the incident and repair the actor's damaged identity.[5]

Looked at this way, apologies perform a healing function. What you want most after some breach is an opportunity for mending what has been torn apart.

As children become older, apologies become increasingly important. Children expect themselves and others to admit responsibility when there has been a transgression. The more a parent acts that way towards the child, the more the child learns about handling mistakes. For example, the parent who barges into his daughter's room without knocking, then apologizes, closes the door, knocks, and begins again is accomplishing several things: Children learn the mechanics of social conventions, that limits are reciprocal, and that their forgiveness counts. When these lessons are learned, mistakes do not seem as dreadful as they might otherwise.

It can also be a powerful help to children during this time for parents to admit some of the mistakes they actually made when they were teenagers. This can be particularly useful to the child who is feeling overwhelmed by self-doubts. Children may have a distorted impression of parents as never having experienced inadequacies similar to the ones that they feel. It is not easy to do, but this sort of exchange can be a welcome gift—admitting that your SAT scores were not dazzlingly high, that you had an automobile accident soon after you got your driver's license, that you used to smoke behind your parents' backs and once messed up the plumbing flushing your secrets down the toilet. The point is not to brag about your peccadilloes, but to share your weaknesses in order to strengthen another's sense that "this, too, shall pass."

The emphasis in this chapter has been on mistakes, as if there were no question about what constituted one. That is far from the case. Parents' notions of mistakes may be children's notions of life experiences. Parents and children often look at the same set of facts and reach very different conclusions; the parent may see a mistake where the child sees a difference in judgment call. For example, parents may think it is a mistake for a daughter to waste her money on going to Florida for spring break. The daughter may think it is money well spent because she wants to be where the action is. Parents may think it is a mistake for a son to decide to become a nurse; the pay and prestige are higher in being a physician. The son may be clear that he is more interested in care than in cure; pay and prestige are not going to rule his life the way they have his parents' lives. Parents may think it is a mistake for a gifted child to bother with study halls. The child may think that some catch-up time is necessary for sanity. Parents may think that their son should not miss his senior prom; he may think that it is a waste of money to take someone when there is no special one in his life right now. Parents may look at a child addicted to computers as antisocial. The child may see this interest as a passion that will pay off career-wise.

Parents want their children to aim as high and as far as possible; anything else may be construed as a mistake. They may feel that they have to keep pushing children to reach their full potential; nothing less will do. It would be a mistake if the child did not grow up to be as strong, good, creative, intelligent, sensitive, warm, and attractive as possible. The problem is that this constant pushing never permits moments when you can be satisfied with yourself. Many times, the push for perfection means that movement which falls short of the ideal is rendered invisible. For example, all the talk about achieving goal weight leaves many a dieter despondent after losing forty pounds because she is still thirty-five pounds from the ideal. What has been accomplished is ignored because the results to date are less than perfect. This way of looking at things often leaves the person wondering whether the struggle is worth it: Why bother? Ultimately, the real mistake may be to live your life never pleased with yourself, and parents play a major role in determining whether their children will be able to take pleasure in what they have done when much remains undone.

If the emphasis is on saving the child, then the parent is the hero of the story. When the focus is on the child's making decisions, then the child is center stage. Can parents ever see their children as competent if they regard every imperfection as evidence of the parents' failing? Will they be capable of complimenting the child on a job well done if they regard themselves as bearing ultimate responsibility for all that happens? This sense of having to save the child, taken to its warped conclusion, can create invisible chains used to bind the child to parents. Fear of mistakes, then, becomes the bogeyman with which to scare the child into submission. The child absorbs the parents' worries and is afraid to venture out in new directions. The child continues to ask, "What should I do?" when he is well past the time when someone else should be setting his agenda.

Paradoxically, the parent's obsession with saving the child from making mistakes can sometimes take so much energy that the parent may have little strength for noticing when things have gone awry. Desperately wanting to avoid all problems can occasionally lead to a denial of difficulties that do exist. For example, the child's growing depression gets dismissed as "only a phase he's going through," even though marked changes have taken place in his sleeping, eating, schoolwork, socializing, and dress (he always wears black). The child's spacy behavior is routinely dismissed as just boredom with school, and the cloyingly sweet smells in the air are not explored as evidence of a drug problem. The child's string of automobile accidents is described as bad luck or bad coordination, and not viewed as self-destructive behavior worth investigating.

To see some problems, you have to be willing to acknowledge that your family is not immune to stress and strain, and that your child can need help without your necessarily having been incompetent as a parent. When her fourteen-year-old started seeing a counselor, one mother was asked, "Do you feel that you've failed as a parent?" Equating the child's need for help with the failure of the parents only makes a mother and father oversensitive about these issues. They are then inclined either to redouble their efforts to prevent problems, usually doing this in a controlling way that is insensitive to children's developmental needs, or to deny that their children have any problems. By the way, the mother who was asked the question said that she did not see going to a counselor as a negative event. She was pleased that her son had recognized a need to talk with someone outside the family about thoughts that were troubling him. To confuse needs with failure would be to misinterpret the situation, and that would be a truly big mistake.

Parents' inclinations to save their children from making mistakes are much more complicated than is usually obvious. If these inclinations have a dark side, they have a bright side, too. Mistakes can be learning experiences for both parents and children. Children learn that making a mistake need not mean the end of their world; that motivates them to try new things. Parents learn that children have an inalienable right to make their own mistakes. Some things cannot be taught through words; they have to be experienced to be thoroughly understood. You both learn that mistakes do not mean that you are a failure; you can fail without being a dud. You learn that you have a commitment to each other that is as resolute in bad times as in good ones. You learn that what first looked like a completely negative event might really be an opportunity to grow and to become tougher and more resilient in the process. Most of all, you learn that unexpected lessons may provide the most enduring learning.

· 6 ·

ONE LAST
SERMON

By the time their children reach adolescence, parents begin to have some sense of time fleeing. It is a combination of being aware that they are at the midpoint in their lives and that their children are more than half grown. The days of bottles, toidey seats, and teething may have seemed fifty hours long, but now the pace has quickened perceptibly. The parent becomes acutely aware of time left. Time is finite; deadlines loom. Is there enough time left to do all the things you wanted to do with your child? Will you get to Disneyland before the child has outgrown interest in such a vacation? Will the moment ever come when you can be comfortable enough to share with your child some of your innermost thoughts and feelings about sex? Will you ever be able to get all concerned together and take a picture of all four generations of women on your side of the family before your grandmother's health worsens? Will you make use of the local state parks before the child hikes out of your life? Will you ever have a holiday with all the trimmings, including a five-course meal using all of the fancy, inherited china that has to be washed by hand?

It is a time of reckoning. Parents confront their unrealized family hopes and aspirations; they examine expectations that they had for their child. Certain marker events force this stocktaking—birthdays, growth spurts, the child moving on from junior high to senior high school, the child getting her first job. You cannot delude yourself that your time living together is open-ended. The remaining days of childhood are down to a precious few, and the parent starts to fret. Your child returns from six weeks at summer camp having an admirer, and you become obsessed with all that she needs to know before going away for a longer time. She has one foot out of the home, and you want to close the door shut and keep her close until you are convinced that she is a finished product.

The parent worries that the child still does not have certain capabilities and qualities. The child does not know how to iron or to play tennis or to use a computer. Chess, changing tires, removing common stains, and knitting remain to be mastered. The child is ignorant of all sorts of maintenance and repair skills. Can she finish off a raveled seam? Can he cook some basics? Does she know that you should check how clean the toilets are before company comes? Does he know that light and dark clothes should not go into the same wash? Does she know how to defend herself if attacked on the street? Better yet, does she know how to avoid dangerous situations? You panic. This child, who always forgets to wear a watch, will never get anywhere on time. This child, who loses everything, will never be able to handle college or a job.

Parents feel guilty about all the times they were too tired or too busy to fit in an after-school activity or family project. They are haunted by school pictures that were never dated, by the baby book that was not kept up beyond the first year. (And it is worse with the second and subsequent children.) Would the children know where Nicaragua and Honduras are located if public affairs had always been the focus of dinner table conversations the way they presumably were in Rose and Joe Kennedy's household? You wish you had read more together;

maybe the child would now have a more extensive vocabulary. Does the child know about the importance of roughage in his diet? If only the violin lessons had begun sooner. Is it too late to teach the child better table manners? If you had gotten into the habit of swimming together at the local gym, could your son have avoided the paunch he now sports? Parents are not totally oblivious of the child's accomplishments, but they tend to be taken for granted. Expectations realized are not often savored; it is those unrealized that prick one's consciousness. Finding their children lacking in certain respects, parents redouble their efforts to prepare them for life. Vacation time becomes an object lesson in geography. Children are lectured once again on the importance of writing "thank you" notes. Newspaper articles on the merits of exercise decorate the refrigerator door. A book on responsible sex is placed on the magazine stack in the bathroom. Children are urged to do more chores in order to learn how to run a household. What the child does not know is so much on the parent's mind that "You mean you don't know . . . ?" becomes the preface to many an exchange. The child feels put down and refuses to let any inexperience show. Once the child's guard is up, the parent redoubles the effort to penetrate the child's defenses and unmask possible shortcomings.

The parent is on a crusade to stamp out ignorance just when the child wants to come into her or his own. The father suggests that the son take golf lessons; the child points out how stupid it is to spend your time hitting a little ball with a stick. The father presses the daughter to sew on some buttons; she swears that she will someday earn enough money to get someone else to do that for her. The mother encourages her son to learn how to cook, and he sings the praises of frozen TV dinners. The mother tells the daughter she should learn how to mow a lawn; she says apartment life is for her. Instead of developing new skills, there are new tensions. Parents are convinced that their children are sassing them, paying no attention. Children resent parents treating them as if they were stupid.

Parents do not usually see their children's refusal to learn something they want to teach in a positive light. But the child's response is more complicated than it seems to be at first glance. It is not necessarily an indication of laziness or impertinence, but may be evidence of initiative, emancipation, and self-determination. The daughter who responds, when her mother insists that she learn to cook by helping her out, by saying, "I don't have to learn everything now; that's why they invented cookbooks," may lack tact, but she does know where to go for information. The child has moved beyond thinking that she has to know everything, to appreciating that a sound understanding of the problem-solving process can help you more in the long run than specific knowledge. A most valuable lesson! There will always be situations calling for skills that you do not have. The issue is whether you know how to proceed when that happens. But how many parents are prepared to applaud such a response?!

Having your premises questioned when all you really want is agreement can be grating, but parents should understand that smart-alecky behavior may be children's way of letting their parents know that they are smart, though not necessarily in the form most appreciated by parents. Teenagers want their parents to recognize how innovative and creative they are. Their arguments may be overly glib, but it helps communication between the generations if you can see the positive side of children's comments. Children sometimes act like show-offs because they want to show off to their parents; they want their applause.

This is a time when children need to see if they can generate a line of reasoning different from their parents. It would be a dull world for them if the older generation had cornered the market on good ideas. On the other hand, it hurts parents to be rebuffed—for that is how it feels—especially if they are offering their children opportunities and resources that were denied to them as children. The parent thinks, I would never have acted so ungrateful if my father had only offered to spend money for me to learn how to _____. It is, of course, a very different situation when you want to do something, as opposed to when you are urged to do something that is not part of your own agenda.

Parents should take comfort, as they worry about how prepared the child is, from the fact that children know how to do more things than they demonstrate on a day-to-day basis. Parents see children not doing certain things, then erroneously conclude that they cannot do them. But children absorb impressions and techniques that may not be put to use right away, but can be drawn on later. For example, the daughter may care nothing for flower arrangement at the age of fifteen, but by watching her mother, may have developed some aesthetic sensibility in that area which can be tapped at thirty-five.

A teenager may be uninterested in carpentry, dressmaking, gardening, and grand-scale entertaining, but may have picked up some pointers just by living with parents who are skilled in these areas. A phone call ten years from now—"Dad, did you always plant marigolds in a border around tomato plants as a way of naturally limiting pests?"—may be needed to access the stored information accurately. Children may not want to admit all that they know because they do not want to be drawn into certain areas. They may not want to be bound by responsibilities for shopping, cooking, and cleaning, but that is different from their having absolutely no awareness of how to perform these tasks.

It is reasonable to expect children to shoulder some household responsibilities, but pushing children to do many jobs just for the experience is bound to elicit a negative response when children do not think that they need the experience. Children shy away from some responsibilities because they do not want to be held accountable in situations where they have no authority. This is particularly the case when parents emphasize that it is "their" house. Often parents expect their children to assume household responsibilities, but will not let them carry these out according to their inclinations and rhythms. They say that they want a job done, then get angry an hour later when it is not done, but they did not say initially that it had to be done in an hour's time. And it did not have to be done that soon. The parent is just testing, and the children are tired of being examined.

When children move out on "their own," they may be eager to remember all those things that they assimilated earlier, but in which they then saw no value. Children not only know what they can show you when you ask, but also have knacks waiting to be developed when the time is ripe for them to become invested in a particular area. They are sponges that have absorbed much, but this saturation may not be visible unless pressed. All that has been incorporated into the person cannot be demonstrated until it is safe to do so—to be clumsy, rough, and unwieldy without editorial comment.

This is a time when parents zealously want to improve the child, but the child may seem even less competent than he once did. When he was nine years old he campaigned to be in charge of mowing the lawn; now that he is sixteen years old it takes hours of pestering to get him to cut the grass. The daughter who was a gourmet cook two years ago, delighting in the creation of desserts that took hours to make, now is reluctant to step into the kitchen. Instead of having some sense of progress, parents may wonder if they are not losing ground. This concern about possible regression causes parents to redouble their efforts to instruct, just when their children are most likely to be upset with being told what to do. The children may be reluctant to keep repeating what they have already learned how to do *(boring!)* because they want to move on to something new. They get very annoyed when their parents act as if they are ignoramuses. It is not so much a matter of whether they can do certain things, but of whether they want to do them. On the other hand, the parents wonder if the child will ever amount to anything since enthusiasms are so short-lived. The generations look at the same behavior, and once again reach different conclusions.

This is a time of reckoning for both generations. Parents worry as much as they do about what their children are lacking because they are assessing themselves as well: Have we been successful at life? Have we been good parents? They are realizing that they can no longer slide by with just being "promising"; this is a time when some of their promise should have been realized. For example, you can be a budding playwright only so long before your potential is expected to bloom. In confronting their own inadequacies, parents may decide all the more to perfect the younger generation. They may also be envious that their children are still full of promise (as opposed to regrets); this may drive them to push their children further "for their own good."

The fact that both generations are dealing with similar issues can be both a disadvantage and an advantage. Children may head towards their high school graduation full of regrets that their childhood was not "more," either because of their own inadequacy or because their family situation was lacking in some respect. Parents may be angry that their children did not handle advantages better or that they themselves have so little to show as a result of the so-called best years of their lives. These sad-angry reflections can lead to bitter recriminations and estrangement, with both generations faulting each other for their regrets.

The other possible scenario is that they can help each other learn to be comfortable with their imperfect lives. It is a case of the old saw: Do you see a half full or a half empty glass? Do parents focus on what they and their children have done or what they have not done? Do they see only that they fell short, or do they also see that they aimed high? If parents can be generally pleased with themselves, despite their faults, that acceptance can transfer to their children. The child who complains, "My parents are never satisfied with anything I do," may have parents who are not satisfied with themselves. If they can accept their children for what they are, however, then they may be less tough on themselves. If parents are accepting, then children are usually more tolerant of their parents, too.

This stocktaking process is expedited by the cognitive ability middle-aged people are likely to have developed not to see situations as either black or white. (Shades of gray can be interestingly textured!) They know, for example, that it is overly simplistic to say that a person is either smart or not. They can recognize different kinds of smartness: book learning, savvy, imagination in different situations, vision. To succeed you need more than a high IQ; you need the ability to get along with people, creativity, a willingness to persevere, and curiosity. These insights can help parents appreciate what they have accomplished even if they were not the smartest persons in their high school class. These same insights can help their children understand that valedictorians and salutatorians are not the only individuals likely to succeed.

Ideally, parents do not sermonize ad nauseam because they appreciate their children for what they are, and know that it is not too late for them to learn new skills, providing they set their minds to do so. They have the attitude that opportunity is open-ended. Instead of pushing their own agendas, they urge their children to decide what they want and how they are going to meet their objectives. What is unaccomplished is viewed largely as a byproduct of an unfinished life. The emphasis is on the child's decision-making, and finding resources so goals can be reached. The parent listens and counsels, but does not act as if her or his opinions are gospel.

This happens ideally, but most parents are far from ideal. They have expectations for what their child should be, and do not easily defer to the child's expectations. They fail to appreciate how much their own expectations have been shaped by personal experience, and may, therefore, be dated as a plan for their child. It is difficult to give up the notion that your son could have been brilliant, handsome, popular, and headed for the Olympics in favor of his actually being good at writing but not at math, awkward but enthusiastic about the tuba, shy but popular with those classmates who are similarly addicted to science fiction, short with big ears, and diabetic. But until you give up stereotyped expectations, you cannot proceed optimistically with what is. You feel cheated, angry, and mourn. You mourn for what was not to be, and miss out on what is.

One of the tasks of this period is to give up any residual expectations that children can be flawless, if parents only do the right thing. This is an imperfect world peopled with imperfect parents and imperfect children, and the challenge is to have expectations that provide direction without browbeating you along the way. Parents regularly feel driven to shape their child into a really outstanding product, only to feel perturbed when they inevitably discover that both generations fall short of expectations. Perfectionistic tendencies resurface with force during the child's adolescence because there is a growing sense that the end to formal parenting is in sight. The child must be as ready as possible for life. Even parents who have felt, up until now, relatively confident about themselves as parents may become riddled with doubts about whether they have done the right thing to ensure their child's future success and happiness. So they may harangue and lecture in a last-ditch effort to squeeze every last idea into their child's head.

Parents do not preach just because they want either to convey large chunks of information or to reel off values that the child should have. There is something about the child's constant questioning that leads parents to want to give answers. The daughter asks, "What do you think?" and the mother feels duty-bound to hold forth. The son is dubious about his mother's values, so she expounds on her beliefs. The daughter points out how dated the father's thinking is, and he defends his position. The father, who once explained that you can always tell which is the left hand because spread out it forms an "L," is used to responding to queries with facts, tips, figures, and opinions. But those are of limited value to the child in this period when questions take precedence over answers.

When children question, they are asking for much more than answers. They want their parents to know that they do not automatically accept as truth everything that is told to them. They are indicating that they are inquisitive, curious, testing, and searching. They are not passive but active. When parents respond with only a string of answers, children feel put in their place, conforming, receptacle-like. They wonder if their struggle for independence is accorded respect, so they struggle anew to run away from their parents' answers, especially those answers that seem unrelated to the original questions.

The parents may see the questioning not as a developmental accomplishment, but as offensive behavior. The child is on the attack. Every verbal sally or shock tactic is regarded as an impertinence. Any dissent gets mistaken for an insult. Rapid-fire comments have a blitzkrieg effect on the parents. They feel beset and besieged, and fall back on sermonizing. The child's behavior puts them on the defensive, so they defend their positions. They feel challenged, so they may become even more opinionated and entrenched in their thinking than usual. They resist the onslaught of questions by hedging, countering, and fighting back. Their children may become more combative after seeing their parents act so guarded. And another cycle of locking horns may get under way.

Endless rounds of attack-defend can be forestalled if parents see their children's sorties as not all requiring answers. If the child says, "I don't believe in God anymore; what do you think of that?," Thomas Aquinas's proofs for the existence of God are not necessarily indicated. Instead of worrying how you are going to get the child to church when grandfather visits at Christmas or feeling guilty about the quality of the religious education you have provided, it makes sense to respond to the introspection that was part of the comment: "Sounds as if you have been giving the matter a great deal of thought. . . . Would you be willing to share with me what brought you to that conclusion?" Children regularly imagine that their parents will only get angry if they are honest about their doubts. It is comforting to know that parents take your musings seriously.

The same thing holds when children say, "What is wrong with abortion?" or any other question that seems to be throwing down the gauntlet for a duel of opinions. Questions are invitations to debate as equals; they are probes to see if the parent is interested in listening to the child's thinking. The parent who automatically responds by quoting chapter and verse may even be seen by the child as too unsure of her or his beliefs to discuss the issues forthrightly. The child wants the parent to speak his own words, no matter how clumsily, so there can be heart-to-heart talk instead of formula conversations. The parent who listens to the child's opinions conveys the unspoken message that this parent's beliefs allow room for the child's thinking, which may make the parent's beliefs ultimately more appealing to the child.

There is evidence that parents' willingness to engage in discussions with teenagers is associated with the children's being more affectionate and respectful towards their parents.[1] The more parents respect teenagers' opinions, involve them in discussions, and explain how they arrive at decisions, the more the young people feel that their parents are people they would "want to be like." If you take children's viewpoints seriously, they are more likely to take your ideas seriously, too. Identity formation is generally thought to be facilitated by family relations that give the adolescent permission to develop her or his own point of view within a context of connectedness.

This way of relating, however, is not necessarily encouraged in American society. Middle-class parents in the United States seem to feel obliged to exercise more control over adolescents and appear to give them less autonomy, not more, than parents in some other Western countries.[2] This may be because the society values a "take charge" style above all else; such chief executives are applauded. A "father knows best" attitude continues to appeal even if a tremendous amount of energy is put into proving how often father does not know what is happening. An increase in the influence of fundamentalist religion has further reinforced the widespread preference for orthodoxy over nonconformity and for strictness over the allowance of dissent. To the extent that parents act as if only they have the right beliefs, then control and defiance become the twin themes shaping exchanges.

When parents refuse to allow the child decision-making opportunities and fail to accept the adolescent's expanding competence, a confrontation can develop in which the parents seek to exert discipline and restrictions that are subsequently viewed by the adolescent as overly rigid and unjust. Parents are domineering, and the child thinks, They've blown it. Why should I do what they want me to do when they neither care about me nor treat me fairly? Adolescent behaviors that were only tentative and experimental become consolidated and entrenched when severely restricted without explanations by parents. Defiance becomes the rule: "You will *not* date him." . . . "Yes, I will; you *cannot* stop me." The more the child resists, the more the parent may seek to set limits, and another round of alienation is under way.

Control issues can also be a feature of different styles of permissiveness. Parents who allow their children to make significant choices when it is convenient for the parents may also believe that they have the right to withdraw decision-making power when they choose; this can lead to anger and resentment on the part of adolescents for such arbitrary and unfair behavior. Parents who are permissive out of indifference often expect their children to place no demands on them; when youngsters do have problems, they may overreact and exert repressive controls.[3] No matter how laissez-faire parents are, they seem to be inclined to reassert control whenever they do not know what else to do. They handle not knowing what to do by telling the child exactly what to do—no ifs, ands, or buts!

American society values people who seem to have the answers. It is no wonder then that parents are quick to give advice, because it is a shorthand way of looking as if you have the answers. Alas, many of the questions teenagers have are ones to which there are either no answers or no simple answers. To the extent that parents keep defending their own viewpoints, oblivious to the fact that there is no one correct answer, they look foolish, obstinate, and calloused. Children dismiss them as inflexible. The parents then feel rejected, and push their positions with the newfound energy of anger and resentment firing them.

Advice tends to be a series of "should" or "should not" statements: You should be contraceptive-minded if you are going to have a sex life . . . You should not drink and drive . . . You should not be promiscuous because venereal disease is on the rise . . . You should do something athletic each semester of college in order to handle stress better . . . You should not tell tales about the family to strangers . . . You should have a bar mitzvah. Advice is the accumulation of a lifetime of experience and can be valuable. But it is the process whereby values were encoded that is more important than any of the individual rules.

Young people seem to recognize that the emphasis should be on values clarification, rather than on commands or directions, months before their parents reach that same conclusion. The parents are so used to the precepts that shape their daily lives that they forget that regulations do not make sense unless you appreciate why and how they evolved. Teenagers reject decrees of any sort; what they are interested in is the rationale behind the maxims. Unless parents are willing to explain themselves and the alternatives that were part of their decision-making process, adolescents do not understand why they should bother to act a certain way.

Children do not want to be mere automatons acting in a mechanical fashion. On the other hand, parents do not think that children are robots when they do what they tell them to do, for what is being told to them is wise. How do parents know it is wise? Because they and others have thought long and hard about these matters. To think long and hard about these matters is, of course, what the children want, in order to see if they reach the same conclusions.

Parents generally want to give to their children. They want to give them the best of everything. Bestowing their accumulated wisdom strikes them as a gift of priceless value. When children seem to reject the advice, the parents feel personally rejected. What they fail to appreciate is that getting advice is like getting a one-page summary of a series which is ten volumes long. You can read the last page, but it seems bloodless and meaningless without the details. More valuable than advice is sharing with children what shaped your thinking.

I personally write with more insight than I live. I have been guilty of sermonizing, oblivious to the fact that I was not making converts. I go off on tangents and bore. I am hurt when my children cut me off midsentence, but I do ramble. I can pontificate in a way that is pompous and off the topic. I admit this in order to point out how difficult it is not to sermonize, even when you disapprove of it. It is easy to get preachy and to become enamored with your own advice, and that is when you leave yourself open to being tuned out or mocked. You can be so intrigued with your ideas that you lose sight of the other person's concerns. You ask a question then answer it yourself. I am particularly likely to fall back on preaching in difficult situations because I want to offer solutions. I want to be Ms. Fix-It. Isn't that what the good mother is?

That tendency to want to fix things and to make them better is a basic part of parenting. In the early years, you fix broken toys and kiss the hurt away. But you do not know how to fix or kiss away peer pressure, incompetent teachers, mood swings, and an unjust society. Instead, you give advice and chide the child for not taking it, in part as a way of still pretending that there are solutions to every problem. You quickly fill the room with your opinions instead of taking the time to *be* for the child. Where once you *did* for the child, parenting in the child's second decade increasingly means being approachable, available, and responsive. You do not hand out one-liners, but are willing to talk things through (which involves more listening than talking). You serve as a sounding board, listening thoughtfully, responding with interest, and asking for elaboration.

This is a time when parents are fully coming to terms with their limits, and children act as catalysts in this process when they constantly remind parents of their limitations. Parents realize that they do not know everything (even if they sometimes pretend); they fall short of their own expectations. Their attitudes, education, prejudices, resources, and opportunities have made them, at most, qualified successes as human beings. Ideally, this midlife appraisal leads to some greater understanding that answers are less important than the questions asked. Indeed, spouting answers can be a way of ignoring complexity in favor of the simplistic. Certainly the world does not just consist of parents who are successful and those who are unsuccessful. It is what these labels have come to represent that needs to be fully considered and explicated. Everyone is a combination of strengths and weaknesses; in fact, some strengths turn out over time to be weaknesses and some weaknesses have a way of turning into advantages. Hopefully, reflecting on the choices they themselves have made leaves parents more prepared to see the limits of any advice-giving, and to give their children more support in striving to reach their own conclusions.

If all parents are inclined to sermonize rather than to be available to their children, this normal tendency is likely to be exaggerated in noncustodial parents. Seeing less of the child, they have less opportunity to have long conversations that do not seem to be getting anywhere, so they often rely on advice as the principal way to shape the child. They are particularly inclined in this direction if they feel caught in a power contest with the ex-spouse as to whose values will take precedence. The child may be more likely to criticize the advice proffered by the noncustodial parent because she or he may begrudge the fact that so many of their precious moments together are spent in this fashion. Hurt and not knowing how to proceed, this parent may give more sermons—this time to the custodial parent: "You tell him . . . I want you to . . . I do not know why you let her. . . ." Both the custodial parent and the child may then decide to present a united defense against the sermonizing, leaving the other parent even more alienated. The problem with sermons is that they leave no room for response, so there is no opportunity for achieving a convergence of opinions.

Some of the advice-giving during the adolescent years is prompted by the assumption that children of this age are still incapable of making important life decisions. The law presumes that parents possess what a child lacks in maturity, experience, and capacity for judgment, though the legislatures of many states have enacted statutes giving adolescents access to and refusal of various types of health care (e.g., contraception and abortion). In fact, it has been demonstrated that adolescents by fourteen do not differ from adults in their capacity to provide competent, informed consent.[4] Still, parents may presume that they have to protect the child well beyond any obvious need to do so. Why? Because they get in the habit of doing so and may want to reserve for themselves some power over the child. It is also true that parents do not always see children at their most competent.

Home is a place where you can collapse after a hard day. The child's neediness may be more obvious in that situation than her or his ability to conceptualize alternatives or to comprehend risks and benefits, so parents may continue to hold dated impressions because they see only one portion of the spectrum of the child's behavior. When parents lament that their child always acts better (or is more pleasant, coping, considerate, sensitive, etc.) with others, they are really noting that the child is accomplished. Alas, these observations may not lead them to treat their child with greater respect because they are so caught up with feeling sorry for themselves. They lash out at the child for not behaving better with them, but they may not try to behave any better with the child. Parents have to ask themselves whether they are not getting what they expect. Does their child continue to act childish with them because they treat him in an infantilizing manner? Parents regularly have to consider whether they encourage sufficiency or pay more attention to incompleteness.

It is not coincidental that this chapter has used language

that conjures up religious images in describing what happens between parent and child during this period—the parent preaches, pontificates, sermonizes, looks for converts. At issue, in parents' minds, is their moral authority. Will they be listened to and treated with respect? This becomes a concern the more children seem to be preferring the company of their peers to that of their parents. This becomes a concern as parents look to the future and wonder what sort of hold they will continue to have on their children. No matter how little the parents formally subscribe to the Judeo-Christian tradition, there is a sense in which all hope that the Fourth Commandment will continue to be enforced. They want their children to honor their mother and father. They want to be treated with consideration and respect. Their probity should be a model for the future.

Parents want to be seen as honorable, but they are also acutely aware of their own faults. They may regret that they have not been more upright, that the religious training of the child was such a jumble of beliefs. Most thinking adults have some doubts about themselves and their values: Should they have been so frank about their misgivings about formal religion? If there had not been such strong insistence on the child's attending Sunday school even when she did not want to, would she now be more committed to the faith of her ancestors? Could the parent have been more exemplary in his behavior? Were the proper values instilled in the child? Should the parents have handled being of different faiths by being unmindful of both?

Parents may be genuinely surprised that they have reached midlife still torn by misgivings. Adults are supposed to be finished products, aren't they? This mix of thoughts and feelings may lead the parent to want to correct any perceived bungling and to elaborate on themes not properly developed, which means another round of lectures and advice-giving. Parents sermonize in the hope both of convincing their children and of finally working out their own beliefs. Children are less likely to see this as a help than as a way of keeping them in their place. The repressive nature of the parents' behavior may impress them more than the supportive element. If they are particularly perceptive, the children may also be annoyed that their parents are so insecure as to be preachy when a lighter touch would carry more weight with them.

Children often accuse their parents of being hypocrites. The parents often push for virtues that they do not possess and profess beliefs that they do not hold. They pay lip service to values that do not guide their own behavior. They expect their children to develop abilities that they long ago gave up trying to master. The children then see them as tricksters, backsliders, and fabricators.

The parents are thinking, Don't do what I do (or did); do what I tell you to do. Even if they did not do well in school, the parents press for good grades from the child. They may be out of shape, but they expect physical fitness in the child. Even though they have spendthrift tendencies, they expect the child to save. Even if they need a martini before dinner every evening, they want a drug-free child. Even though they cannot stand bugs, they want a child comfortable in the great outdoors. Even if they despise their bosses, they want a child who has no problems at work. They may be addicted to coffee and diet sodas, but they want a child free of caffeine and artificial sweeteners. Even though their hair is bleached, they want a child who does not dye her hair and risk dry ends.

The children see their parents as hypocrites because they do not practice what they preach. The parents see themselves as just wanting more for their children than they have been able to obtain in their own lives. They do not see this as a sham; it is just being responsible. Their children may accuse them of insincerity, but the parents are sincere in wanting their children to get things right, even if it has proven difficult or impossible in their own lives. They review their lives to date, then use some of the unfinished business in their own lives to set their children's agendas. What they need to do is give up expecting inhuman perfection in themselves, so they can give up expecting inhuman perfection in their children.

Diana Baumrind is an acknowledged expert on the relationship between styles of parenting and their consequences on children's behavior. She has followed families over time and has formed her own opinion about which aspect of the Judeo-Christian tradition should direct parenting in order to develop competence in children. She found that successful "authoritative" parents, in contrast to unsuccessful "authoritarian" parents, believe they should be receptive to, and aware of, the child's needs and views before making any attempt to alter the child's actions. They set standards and enforce them firmly but do not regard themselves as infallible; they value obedience to adult requirements, as well as independence in the child. They prize the norm of reciprocity, "Do unto others as you would have them do unto you," one of the greatest commandments.[5] This reciprocity presumably leaves both generations more understanding of each other's struggles.

The title of this chapter does not just conjure up religious images, but also suggests that a sense of finality shapes parents' behavior. Parents are approaching some final point, so all goals should be achieved. Everything should be certain; all answers should be in; a sense of completeness should be realized. The end is in sight; the finishing stroke waits to be applied; the final exam is about to be taken.

It is understandable that parents are driven by some sense that this is their last chance to be all that a parent should be. At the midpoint of life, they feel as if it is "now or never" for them personally, and for them as parents. They may look towards their children's high school graduation as a graduation of sorts for them. They may become obsessed with the "last" family vacation, the "last" big Thanksgiving, the "last" free time before the job begins, the "last" summer before college. Expectations mount, only to be toppled by their enormity and exaggeration. A self-consciousness develops; photographs have to be taken before this moment evaporates. Everyone assumes poses; relations are stilted. No one acts very well; hope sours into apprehension. The child, so loved by the parents, begins to feel unwelcome. If this is the "last" major family picnic, the future seems empty, wanting, and unsettled. In this view, "growing up" means giving up past relationships, not taking on new ways of relating. Losses are emphasized more than gains. Tempers flare, and both generations wish they were done with each other.

Middle age is not the end of possibilities, and adolescence is not the end of special parent-child relations. Change can be for the good of all. The child's coming into her or his own can mean that parents can come into their own in a new way. This may involve deciding to do for themselves some things they wanted for their children. Instead of sticking their children with their ambitions, they can realize their own ambitions. The memories shared and the embraces exchanged will always be there to be remembered and to be extended. The drive to have the last word only makes conversations bog down; you wind up remembering what you said but not the other person's response. A swan song is a monologue; what you really want is an ongoing dialogue. That means parents do not always have the last word.

· 7 ·

A TASTE
FOR VENGEANCE

No matter how much sense you try to make of the second decade of parenthood, there is an element to the experience that is far from reasonable. The issues of that period can be understood only against a backdrop of intense feelings. One mother described her relationship with her daughter as that of two sumo wrestlers locked in a deadly grip on a desolate, dry-ice landscape. This mother spoke with intense pride later in the conversation about her daughter's emergence as a young woman of grace, talent, and sensitivity. Such a loving tribute would seem to be incompatible with the image of searing combat, yet both representations are part of the maelstrom of feelings that characterize those years.

This is a period of "normal crazy" feelings. "Normal crazy" refers to those emotions and thoughts that deviate from what the literature and public opinion regard as ideal or appropriate behavior. Yet you know most people experience them after spending countless hours collecting anecdotes and prevalence statistics over coffee and in cocktail party laboratories. The feelings and thoughts are normal in that most people have them, even if most do not rapidly admit to being so torn or extreme for fear of being described as having a crazy streak.

What are some examples of "normal crazy" thoughts and feelings? Siblings who always seemed to be arguing with each other go out for pizza together and return home giggling. Instead of rejoicing in this miracle, the father feels left out and wonders if he is not the butt of their joke. The mother, who never wanted to be as irrational as her own mother seemed to be, answers the request, "Can I go over and visit with Bob?" with "I suppose you like him better than us." The father who swore that he would never lose his cool, gives a lengthy monologue on how self-centered his son is, even though the child is generally helpful when asked to do things. The mother yells about being treated like a maid, even though she never asks her daughter to assume responsibility for her own laundry. Parents sometimes seem more comfortable quarreling about the existing order than reordering matters.

Parents are touchy. As their children become independent, they may feel left behind. They may feel used, ignored, and unappreciated. Some children may strike out on their own, and treat home only as a place for getting clean clothes and for raiding the refrigerator, but parents tend to have negative feelings even when their children have not been particularly contrary or distant. If their children have done poorly in school or have gotten into trouble, they obviously may feel disappointed and aggrieved. But they can also feel negative when their children achieve the extraordinary. The brilliant daughter may remind her father that his potential has not been fully utilized. The handsome son may remind his mother that her own good looks are sagging. The athletic daughter may remind her father that his endurance is not what it once was. The entrepreneurial son may remind his mother that she will never be as rich as she once dreamed of becoming. The parent who is between jobs may resent the beginning salary of a newly graduated child.

The air is charged. The children strut their stuff. The parents watch them, wishing they were Greek gods of old who could either hurl thunderbolts when their children displeased them or freeze their movements outside time. The children see that their parents are not the mythic figures they once believed them to be; the parents miss what little hero worship there once was.

Feelings are intense and need decoding. Comments often say more about what the parent is feeling than about what the child is doing. The father who snickers, "The ice bitch has deigned to give us the pleasure of her company," feels cut off from his child. The mother who mutters about her daughter's being so wrapped up in herself that she would never notice if she were hemorrhaging to death is commenting on how ignored she feels. The father who needles his son about his sexual adventures (or lack thereof) may envy him possibilities he never had or may mourn the waning of his own libido. The mother who yells, "Don't you think you can lord it over me just because you are six inches taller than I am," is worried that she may be disregarded. The parent who complains about a child's moodiness may be wondering, Why aren't you happy? I have done everything I could think of to try to please you.

No pale pink or baby blue feelings are these. They are not the delicate and mellow portion of the spectrum, but the florid. They are raw, stark, harsh, and shrieking. The intensity may shock. Young people can be irascible, sullen, volatile, and explosive; the parents may find the seesawing of their own feelings equally riotous and unsettling.

The feelings may seem to be unreasonable, but there are reasons for these emotional cloudbursts. The parents are wondering whether parenthood was worthwhile. They feel as if the child has squeezed affection, time, and money out of them, leaving them drained and wrinkled. They may have become parents so they could give love and be loved, but now the child shudders at the approach of a hug and may not even want to be seen walking with her parents. Gone are the days when Mother's Day or Father's Day meant a wonderful assortment of heart-shaped bookmarks, flower-pasted coasters, or small handprints encased in plaster. Now it may be a disdained last-minute obligation rather than an occasion for sentimental celebration. Even parents who themselves have long criticized the commercial nature of the obligation may now want some doting acknowledgment that their child feels obligated.

Just about all of the advantages cited for having children may seem not to hold during the second decade of parenthood. Teenagers sometimes seem to be clinging to their friends and avoiding your company, so the role of children in warding off loneliness or providing companionship may seem minimal at this time. Whatever their original value may have been in providing fun and stimulation, their disconcerting antics may now leave you uncomfortable rather than distracted from your troubles. Instead of providing present life with meaning and purpose, teenagers may spend hours questioning the meaning of their parents' lives, leaving them feeling deprived of purpose. Any sense of obtaining vicarious achievement may be thwarted when the parent is not satisfied with the child's efforts. The possible economic utility of the child may not be obvious when you contemplate the cost of college.

Parents often feel unappreciated at this time. What they have done for the child may seem to go unnoticed, but any failing is quickly pointed out to them. Not only may their sacrifices be taken for granted, but the children may regard being reminded of them in any way as unforgivably tacky. The child wants to be positively reinforced, but may not think to do the same for his parents. The parents are tempted to hurl ugly words at the child: ingrate, leech, slut, barbarian, hood, bum, monster. The parents imagine the child will never lift a hand to take care of them when they are old and ailing. Parents have rich imaginations; they can easily picture a thankless, unrewarding future extending endlessly before them.

Parents feel misunderstood. The daring and silly parts of them have been progressively sealed over by a series of responsibilities. Those inclinations are dormant, not extinguished. The child refers to you as an "old fogy," and you resent being described as old-fashioned, when it was for the sake of the child that you assumed a mature attitude. You are cautious out of a sense of duty. The true you, which can be defiant, ebullient, and imaginative, is overlooked by the child. You have become part of the caricature called parents, and your peculiarities have been exaggerated to produce a comic, grotesque effect. The child is so bent on proving that he is an interesting, exceptional person that your own individuality gets ignored. Parents regularly feel sorry for themselves, in part, because they do not think that anyone else really appreciates their situation.

The child has one foot out the door and the parents may want to slam it shut. Hold on to the child; who cares if the foot gets a bit squashed?! Holding on may seem to be the only sensible response at this time when a sense of loss may be the predominant motif. You fear a growing sense of discontinuity; the numbers at home are shrinking. But many other losses seem intertwined with the child's growing up and away. The best man at your wedding dies, the first one of your own generation to go. You feel choked by responsibilities to childless aunts and elderly neighbors. Your own parents fail. You care for them as best you can, wishing that you could do more, but convinced that your child may not do as much for you. You may become an orphan; a forty-seven-year-old orphan is still an orphan. You feel cut off; there is no one ahead of you. You are the next in line and feel very vulnerable.

Your body ceases to be your friend. Your blood pressure is up and your energy is down. Your upper arms are Jello-O soft, and you swear off sleeveless dresses. The print gets smaller and you consider bifocals. You wonder what is in Grecian Formula, and if it works. The dentist sighs when he looks into your mouth, and says you had better cap the upper right section because it is crumbling more quickly than expected. The knees hurt when you go up and down the steps. All the laugh lines that web your face make you want to cry. Getting up, after sitting on the floor, is a clumsy struggle. Liver spots march, in dirge rhythm, across your hands. You feel depressed, dispossessed, and bereft.

You are scared of growing old, of dying. You thought that you would have come to terms with these issues long before this, and you have not. You still catch yourself thinking in terms of "if I die," not "when I die." You may hate attending wakes and funerals, but it is less easy to avoid them because more of your friends and relatives are in the upper-age group. You begin to wonder how your obituary will read, and you realize that you still have not accomplished many of the things that you want written about you.

You are scared of what life will be like without the crutch of having children at home. If you have been a stay-at-home mother, you may be scared of becoming redundant now that the adolescent no longer obviously needs you. All those excuses that you made, naming the children as the reason you could not do something you did not want to do, will soon be no more. Will you do what you said you would do once the children were launched—move elsewhere, go back to school, get another job? Or will you lose your nerve?

If you are married, you may be scared of becoming a couple once again. When you have restored to you all the privacy that you could want, will you want to make love more, or will you be sorry to have lost your excuse for a sluggish libido? All those times when the two of you acted more as partners in a company, rather than as lovers, leave you wondering whether you can handle a return to intimacy. When the noise has turned to silence, will you speak endearments or realize that there is more form than substance to your relationship? If you have stayed together "for the sake of the children," then their emancipation means decision time.

You feel generally angry, too. Angry at Brooke Shields stuffed into designer jeans. Angry about the hickey you noticed on your daughter's neck when she returned home from a date. Angry that you missed the sexual revolution. Angry that your fifteen-year-old daughter was given a dozen long-stem roses by an admirer before you ever were. Angry at all the teen movies peopled by idiot parents and cunning children. Angry that your child has advantages you never had, and does not appreciate them. Angry that mirrors are prejudiced against the older woman when you ask of them, "Who is the fairest one of all?" Angry that your teenage stepdaughter is so bitchy and seductive. Angry that there are fewer actors of your age on television, and those featured seem to be capable of doing only hemorrhoid commercials. Angry that your child distinguishes between "his world" and "your world"—olden days.

Most of all, you may be upset that instead of becoming a role model to your child (the subject of admiration), you have come to represent much of what she does not want to become (the epitome of what is to be avoided). You scrimped and saved because you did not want your family to be as poor as you were growing up, and your son vows never to fret about every dollar the way you have. You struggled to be a man of principle, and your son says principles are a luxury item in today's job market. You made an effort to be honest and open about your feelings, since your parents always masked theirs, and your daughter becomes phlegmatic because she does not want to become as quick to tears as you are. You worked to become a success, hoping to prove to your daughter that women can be anything they want to be, only to be told that she does not want to have a career after watching you sweat blood. Or you put your own career plans on hold for the sake of the children, only to be told by them that you are an anachronism and that they do not intend to waste their time raising children. Such apparent repudiation can be especially difficult for adoptive parents and stepparents who may feel that they have gone the extra mile to be a positive influence.

No amount of reasoning about how normal it is for children to be critical of parents—it is one way to prove their independence—can take away the sting of not being appreciated for what you are by your own. Teenagers seldom understand the context of their parents' lives; they do not even understand themselves. Still, parents feel repudiated. Even if they remember having been critical of their own parents, they cling to the hope that it will be different with them. (That is, of course, what their children are thinking, too: It will be different with them.) Slapped in the face (or so it seems), parents resort to becoming offensive themselves. If their children can snipe at them, they can give as good as they get, even better. And they do.

Biblical imagery plays a part in shaping parents' thoughts and feelings, even if they themselves are not particularly religious. All those allusions to God as a benign parent who meets His children's needs go hand in hand with His being a divinity who does not tolerate disobedience lightly. Rewards, justice, fruitfulness, and long life are predicated on submission to the authority who knows what is best for you. Abraham has the right to sacrifice Isaac. God does not require this death once His power has been confirmed, but the message is clear: Children, submit to your parents as they, in turn, yield to the Lord. The authority of parents is godlike; their right to retribution is legitimate.

There is something about children criticizing their parents, even if the parents have a long history of criticizing their children, that unleashes a taste for vengeance in them. Parents are capable of exquisite putdowns. The son may want to start shaving, and the father may gleefully tell him (frequently in front of others) that there is no need for him to do so when all he has is peach fuzz. The mother may constantly remind her stout fifteen-year-old daughter that she weighed a mere 104 pounds until she married at twenty-five. Every mistake can be greeted with a chorus of "I told you so!" Then there are the cultural putdowns that go well beyond individual annoyance: The coffee mug that says, "Insanity is hereditary; you get it from your children." The apron that proclaims, "Mother Nature, in all her wisdom, gave me 13 years to love my son before making him a teenager." The poster that reads, "The first half of life is ruined by our parents; the second half by children."

Parental fears and anxieties reach an all-time high during their children's adolescence, and so does the competition called "Can You Top This?" Parents who ordinarily would not think of airing their troubles in public boastfully trade horror stories about their teenagers as if they were accumulating points towards some prize. A father describes how his son ruined one car and is working on doing the same to another. A mother recounts that her high school daughter is sleeping with a mindless Adonis. (If a bystander would join in this putdown of their children, he is likely to be put in his place; as with all intense relationships, only intimates are allowed to disapprove.) The children are perceived as uncontrollable; pride, envy, love, sexuality, wonder, and hate are all mixed together. It is as if the parents want others to compliment them for demonstrating grace under fire. Is the complaining meant to elicit sympathy from others when none is coming from the children? Is the listener being invited to say that the behavior is only normal? I know I revert to calling my children "kids"—a word they hate since they are not goats—when I am talking about them with friends. It is a word that puts distance between my children

and me. As my older daughter once said, "Mom, are you trying
to impress?" But what is the impression parents want to
make? That they can take their children or leave them (now
that they have reached a time when their children can take
them or leave them)?

Another way parents put their children down is by constantly telling them that they have no problems or that the
ones they have are petty: "You think you have troubles; just
wait until you're my age. Then you'll know what real problems
are." The children know how miserable they sometimes feel,
and do not understand why their own experience is often discounted. Only their parents' problems seem to be accorded respect. Yet it can be a catch-22 situation: Children will never be
the same age as their parents, so parents will always be ahead
of their offspring, disregarding their complaints and demanding sympathy for their own, on the grounds that the children
cannot truly understand with what the parents have to
contend.

Constant reminders that "these are the best years of your
life" can further alienate children. The message communicated
is that it is all downhill from now on, not a viewpoint that
leaves you eager to embrace the future. There are other strategies aimed at killing the spirit: "A hard day's work would kill
you" (impugning the child's industry and motivation); "Compared to my childhood, yours is a piece of cake" (asking for
sympathy, but giving none to the younger generation); "After
all I have done for you" (implying that the score can never be
settled and mutuality is impossible); and "I am doing this for
your own good" (giftwrapping some anger and carping).

To understand parents' feelings, you have to appreciate the
extent to which parents want to be loved without question.
They want life to be like the Geritol commercial in which the
daughter says, "Mom, you're incredible!" They want their children to know that they have done the very best that they

could, to appreciate their efforts, and to have happy memories of their childhood. They want affection, devotion, and respect. Rearing children was to have been an affirmation of their generosity, tenderness, and nobleness. The task would be complicated and difficult, but the rewards would be palpable—kisses, shared fun, a sense of solidarity. Even if they remember once wanting to run away from their own parents, they probably continue to regard any estrangement between the generations as the exception rather than the rule. Such a position is reinforced by all those newspaper articles and magazine stories that describe how to be an effective parent.

Does all this sound dreadfully naïve? Yes, but that is because you are always somewhat naïve about new situations. Most parents are surprised by the process of separation, with its attendant emphasis on dissent and nonconformity. To the extent that parents expect contrariness, they may envision it as always ending in eleventh-hour agreement. All the literature on the link between attachment and positive feelings in the early years leaves parents unprepared to equate letting go with being enthusiastic about the child. There is relatively little discussion of these matters in the childrearing literature, so parents react (and overreact) to the child's struggle for self-determination. Disagreement feels like disapproval; questioning feels like repudiation; letting go feels like loss.

The child's struggle to become her or his own person is especially difficult for parents with shaky self-esteem (and everyone's shakes at times). In having a child they may have hoped to achieve self-fulfillment; this would be the one completely affirming relationship. Feeling this way, they may have a history of looking to the child for approval. When the child ceases to be attentive to the parents' wishes, they may feel doubly distraught. The support is gone, and in its place is another difficult relationship. Feeling unappreciated, parents are disinclined to respond to the child with understanding.

It is impossible for parents not to have mixed feelings about their children growing up, even in the best of relationships. Childless individuals can more easily avoid thinking about growing old, but parents naturally equate their child's growing up with their own growing old. Arguments about how the middle-aged are not old and how the empty nest frees parents to try new things, can comfort, but they cannot erase the link. If your descendants ascend, what happens to you? The parents may come to resent their children's youth. Any hassle gets interpreted as "These children are responsible for my hair turning white overnight" or "These children will be the death of me." This attitude when expressed just makes the children want to keep their distance from parents who seem so illogical and fanatical.

The strong negative feelings are an expression of the firm bond already in place between the generations. Most parents care so much about their children that every tug on the connection is felt. They resist any loosening of the tie and hold on tight; it is a reflex action. Love is so equated with feeling close that any parting of company is mistaken for disaffection.

If there are so many turbulent feelings during this period, what can you do about them? Can you exorcise these devilish emotions, or do you just have to live through them? Ugly feelings often seem beyond reason, but it is important to realize that they may be the consequence of how you think about things. You cannot simply will anger and envy away, but change your thinking about an event and you can influence how you feel about that event.

Cognitive appraisals play an important role in the experience of emotion. Different explanations are associated with different feelings. For example, when individuals want to achieve at parenting, think they should be able to succeed, but fail for reasons that they do not quite understand, they are likely to feel frustrated. To the extent that they perceive that someone else (e.g., the child) is preventing them from reaching their objective, the prevailing emotion may be anger. If, on the other hand, the impediment is due to uncontrollable forces (e.g., sickness, financial constraints), the emotional response may be sadness.[1]

It has been demonstrated generally that the explanations you make for an event also have consequences for subsequent expectations and behaviors.[2] For example, if you explain a child's contrary behavior as unchanging then you are likely to expect the same thing to happen again and again, and to act accordingly. There are many times when parents explain their children's behavior as fixed, when it is only a function of their developmental stage. These unfounded conclusions can then become self-fulfilling prophecies because the parents act "as if" those expectations were true. For example, parents assume that their child cannot handle money because he once used all of his allowance to buy something frivolous; they treat him as careless, not allowing him opportunities to manage resources, then find him lacking in that critical area because he has been deprived of opportunities to learn how to improve.

The explanations that are most likely to leave you feeling positive about the child involve attributing accomplishment to internal qualities (e.g., the child did well in math because she is good in that area, rather than because she lucked out) and failure externally (e.g., the child acted loud and obnoxious because she was responding to group pressure, rather than because she is loud and obnoxious). Explaining performance in terms of fixed factors means that you expect the success or failure to be repeated, all other things being equal. It may be comforting to think that a child has the personality to succeed, but intrinsic traits should be used sparingly as an explanation for lack of success. The child who is still figuring out "Who am I?" is in process. His flaws and foibles should be understood within the context of developmental changes taking place. Not every failure or tension can be written off as "just a phase he is going through," but it is a disservice to the child when parents ignore this simple explanation and instead overgeneralize the negative.

Parents seem inclined to overgeneralize—for example, the child does not go along with something her father wants her to do, then regularly gets described thereafter as not respecting her elders. They see one or two instances of behavior, then conclude that this will be true evermore, unless they do something to modify the behavior. They go in with heavy artillery to extinguish the culprit behavior only to find that their inclination towards overkill has made the situation worse. The child challenges one cherished belief, and the mother concludes that he wants to topple all of her beliefs. The child chides the father for being elitist on a particular day, and he concludes that she is convinced that his personality is flawed. There is a "normal paranoia" to which parents are prone that leads them to show some unreasonable distrust and suspicion. This, in turn, generates a wariness in the child, which can lead to another round of the parents' feeling persecuted.

The intense desire parents have to be loved by their children, coupled with society's negative attitude towards teenagers, leaves parents likely to pay particular attention to any negative behavior.[3] One sarcastic remark gets interpreted as a trend. The child makes ten neutral statements, pays three compliments, and says something biting. What does the parent notice? The biting remark, of course. The child thinks her uncaring parent is always ready to think the worst of her, and is hurt. The parent cares so much for the child that he fixes on anything that interferes with his idyllic view of parent-child relations.

The child makes a callous remark, and the parent concludes that the child has a calloused personality. Because the child is sullen or abrupt one week, the mother imagines her son acting that way in the months, years, and decades ahead. She chides him for turning into a brat; he sees her as overly censorious. The relationship becomes like tinder in a way that could have been avoided if the original behavior had been viewed within a particular context, not as an example of a general rule.

Parents can overgeneralize feelings by using an extreme descriptor when a less loaded one is more accurate. You wind up feeling very different if you say, "She hates me," instead of, "She is annoyed with me." Negative-feeling tones need not indicate hate. All relationships are full of transitory annoyances without love necessarily being imperiled. A person can be stern, crusty, crabby, sulking, cross, and grouchy without hate being an issue. Oddly enough, it is the parents' powerful desire for love that makes them quick to examine every sour exchange for evidence of hate. And when they conclude that their child hates them, they themselves may turn hateful, with disastrous consequences for the relationship.

How you explain matters shapes how you feel about them. For example, if you describe an exchange with your daughter, who said your penchant for black suits makes you look funereal, as a putdown, you feel one way. If you describe the same situation as an indication of her being grownup enough to be fashion-conscious, you feel another way. If your son's gaggle of friends is considered proof that he is not interested in his family, you feel one way. If the same details are considered evidence of his popularity and ability to get along with people, you feel another way. One person's notion of rebellion can be someone else's notion of independence. Disagreement that can signal conflict to one parent, may be seen as an ordinary part of serious conversation by another parent. It is interesting to speculate on whether adolescence varies so much from child to child, or whether parents vary in their interpretations of similar behaviors. It has been suggested that "the level of interfamily stress may be elevated due to the discrepant perspectives of parents and their adolescents regarding family issues and dynamics,"[4] so it may be that families per se do not vary as much as whether members draw similar conclusions about the same events.

Overgeneralizing is especially deadly during this period because children may feel in such a state of flux that they do not know just who they will be tomorrow. Rebellion at fifteen is part of a developmental process, but that does not mean that the child will have the same need to be contrary at the age of twenty-five. The child is changing, as she or he strives to become a self-contained person. Once the escape from dependency is achieved, the child will be able to show soft, warm feelings to his parents again without having to worry that they will be able to hold him in check with those ties of affection. With some distance—geographic, chronological, emotional— the child will have a new perspective on his parents. For example, it is not unusual for children returning home from college to have a new appreciation of their parents, particularly if their parents notice how grownup they have become since going away.

Children will never wholly understand their parents (as parents will never wholly understand their children), but they are likely to understand them better over time. Parents have to take the long view during their children's adolescence. The struggle for identity means that parents have to be set aside in some sense, but that is so the children will be in a better position to connect with them in the future. Unless parents can appreciate that letting go in the present does not necessarily mean emotional distance in the years to come, they are likely to hold on in a way that damages the relationship. Letting go of their control over the adolescent is paradoxically the way the parents remain attached.[5]

Letting go is difficult, so some parents bind their children to them with guilt. Independence is sometimes applauded, but it is sometimes regarded as wrongdoing. The parents find letting go offensive, so they treat it occasionally as an offense. The mixed messages leave the child feeling unsure and guilty, but also angry that he never seems to suit them. It is as if the parents can remain comfortable only by keeping the child in place. The child retaliates by complaining about how bored he is: His parents never let him do anything. He wants to get away from home to find a new way of relating. The hours seem leaden where sameness is the rule. The child's laments about tedium and stodginess put the parents on the defensive. Guilt . . . Boredom . . . Guilt . . . Boredom . . . is the background beat.

The parents are so inclined to overgeneralize that they see only differences where there are also similarities. A son decides not to be confirmed because he is not ready to make a commitment of faith, but sings loudly at the service with a large silver cross around his neck. Do you focus on the refusal or the prominent wearing of a religious symbol? A daughter dresses unconventionally, but combines on her person a jacket and skirt from her mother's college days and rhinestone jewelry bequeathed by a great aunt. Do you focus on how outlandish the costume is or on the continuity implicit in building her style on favorite attic treasures?

Overgeneralizing is also problematic when parents connect several events, as if they belonged together, then treat them as part of one phenomenon. It is especially unfair to the child when the death of grandparents, disappointment at not getting an expected promotion at work, beginning arthritis pains, and the child's launching become intertwined. Each event may lead to a sense of loss, but those events are not causally linked. The mind is not always logical, and may see patterns where there are none just because these events took place during the same period. However, relations between the generations are bound to be strained if you act as if the child's emergence into adulthood were responsible for your mourning or your ailing.

One of the impossible expectations that parents have, which encourages negative feelings, is that their children will be happy. Though their own lives may never have included periods of moo-cow contentment, they expect their children to feel that way. Having them as parents was supposed to mean honor-roll grades, freedom from disease, and a life without moods, doubts, and fussiness. It sounds preposterous when said aloud, but until parents recognize such preposterous tendencies in themselves, they have difficulties dealing with their children when they are not happy. The child's unhappiness, instead of being regarded as an inevitable part of the human condition, is an occasion for the parents to feel unsuccessful and to fuss: "What is the matter with you?" Alas, parents who feel unsuccessful are inclined to get angry with the child: "Given what you've had, any other child would be grateful, ecstatic, and overjoyed." That is not true, but it is difficult for the child, still relatively new to the human condition, to question such logic when supposedly mature adults still subscribe to such views.

Negative emotions are like physical pain; they let you know what is going on inside you. You will never be able to stop having these feelings, but you should appreciate their diagnostic value. They are telling you something about your expectations. For example, you cannot be disappointed without having some thwarted expectations, even if you cannot readily articulate them. This period, rich in feelings, should be regarded as an opportunity to come to terms with leftover unreasonable expectations. Do you still expect unquestioning obedience (even though you have never tendered or received it)? Do you expect the child to be even-tempered even though both parents have rather tempestuous temperaments? Do you expect the child to get along with everyone, yet always be true to herself? Do you expect parents to have most of the answers? Do you expect to be always right?

All adolescents, like all adults, will sometimes demonstrate bad manners, hurtful remarks, and thoughtless actions. They will "constructively criticize" their parents' behavior, as they have experienced their parents doing the same to them, with sometimes crushing results. As they leave childhood behind, young people are inclined to rethink their past, and their evaluations may not always be kind. When censured, the parent's response is likely to be similar to that described by the therapist David Elkind: "Psychologist or not, I was sorely tempted to use physical abuse to express my reaction." The best antidote for such a response, in his estimation, is not to wait to comment on the hurt, lest it fester: "Young people have to learn that whereas physical hurts go away in time, those caused by words can last a lifetime. If we don't speak up about our feelings, we only harbor and build up our anger for an uncontrolled explosion later."[6]

That is good advice. Parents have the responsibility of letting the child know when a cutting remark has pained them. You do not want them to get in the habit of thinking that they can hurt others without consequences; that is not a preparation for the real world. But the principal reason parents should respond when such a remark is made is so that unexpressed feelings do not build into a violent explosion weeks later which makes no sense to the child.

One of the major tasks parents have to learn during this period is not to retaliate with full force when children aim for parents' areas of vulnerability and insecurity. The inclination is to let the child have it with both barrels; if maximum retaliation is used, the hurtful remark will be annihilated for all time. There is a tendency to forget that the child might be wiped out in the process.

Especially if their anger is more than justified, parents may feel that they can retaliate with impunity. They assume that anyone capable of such sting should be able to withstand a counterattack. What they fail to realize is that the forces are unequal. Parents may think otherwise, but children are more likely to be devastated by their parents' anger than parents are likely to be hurt by that of their children, if for no other reason than that parents have had more experience with life's ups and downs. Family members exert tremendous power over each other, both for good and for evil. They know what will hurt; they know how to aim right for the heart. Parents have to demonstrate by their example that this is not a power with which you toy. You do not use response number 10 when response number 2 will do!

Most adults reach their children's adolescence without having learned all that much restraint. In relationships with peers, for example, you do not feel compelled to serve as a role model. But in dealing with your children's struggle to become independent, you have to consider whether you are willing to endure some (normal) carping and criticism without either falling apart yourself or striking out at the source. Fury never convinced anyone to act humanely, but having a sense of humor about the situation may.

One of the best things you can do during these years is to cultivate your funnybone. When you respond to your child's listing of grievances with, "You've got my number; you should be an accountant," you are clearing the air without getting bogged down in lengthy justifications of your behavior. When you point out a child's error in judgment by saying, "You're not supposed to do that; you're supposed to be perfect," the crazy part of expectations is also being acknowledged. When you remind your child to be kind to grownups—"They have some good points; they try hard"—you are asking for consideration in a way that is not full of recriminations. "Humor me; pretend I know something you don't know" is a way of asking that your opinions be respected without being self-righteous.

Humor that does not make the other person the butt of the joke has a cathartic effect; it reduces tensions. Criticisms and mistakes can be acknowledged without war being declared. There is a great deal to laugh at when parents expect their children to become interesting individuals without ever criticizing their parents, and when children set out to shock their parents out of the old ways of relating. When parent and child can laugh together at their foibles, they are demonstrating that they are willing to humor each other—that is, to be tolerant of each other's position.

The best revenge parents have is not the slap or the curse, but being able to say, "Don't be too hard on me; I didn't do so badly. Look at how well you turned out." That way children learn that they cannot repudiate you without repudiating a part of themselves. Anyway, repudiation is not what growing up is all about; the task is to embrace the future even though your past was not perfect.

Optimally, both parents and children come out of this period with some sense that this was a "good-enough" family.[7] Neither the parents nor the children were perfect. They both had faults, but none were so large that they obliterated the capacity for good times. With distance, some of the hassles and responses will seem silly—the stuff of which funny stories at family gatherings are made. Still, the family was good enough to produce a cast of characters good enough for remembering and loving.

· 8 ·

ROOTS

AND WINGS

In the second decade of parenthood, the mother and father have to let go of earlier notions of what it means to encourage the growth and development of their children. Where once the emphasis was on cuddling, safeguarding, instructing, admonishing, improving, and caring for, now encouraging the child to come into her own takes precedence over making her your own. The first decade is a time for teaching the child a long list of basics, from dental hygiene to moral principles. By contrast, the second decade of parenthood is a time when the child questions those values, and, in the process, makes them his own: Do I brush my teeth because my mother is looking over my shoulder and expects me to do so, or because *I* want to do so? . . . I know what my father thinks, but what do *I* think about premarital sex? The child no longer automatically submits to his parents' wishes, but increasingly decides for himself what approach to take. Both children and parents are in a transition period: Parental authority is no longer *the* operating rule, but the emphasis has not yet moved either to parents' always respecting the separateness and maturity of their children or to the children's being ready for emotional separation and complete financial independence.

This period is one of metamorphosis. The child sprouts up, becomes self-assertive, and may leave home for good by the end of his high school years. The parent may be uncomfortable with each of these movements. Physical changes may evoke all sorts of feelings in the parent, from feeling that the sweet, beloved child has been replaced by a tempestuous, sexy stranger, to a sense that the child is now literally and figuratively looking down on the parent. Self-assertion may often feel like repudiation of the parents and what they represent. The prospect of moving away from home signals the coming end of an era; the child will soon no longer need his parents' support on a day-to-day basis.

If parents find the second decade of parenthood difficult, there are solid reasons why that is the case. A parent does not have to be inept nor a child perverse for this to be an exacting and baffling time. The very fact that society makes a fuss over young children, but expects teenagers to make a fuss, indicates the negative mind-set so many have about this period.

Many of the reasons for this attitude have already been discussed. One of the major reasons that this is a difficult time is because there are no set guidelines for dealing with adolescents comparable to those available for the younger years. Although the infant is much more complicated than was previously thought (e.g., the newborn can respond in kind to facial expressions), there are still a limited number of possibilities to the child's behavioral repertoire. If you understand something about the infant's needs for nourishment, language interaction, impulse control, stimulation, consistency, and safe opportunities to move about, then you can be adequate to the tasks at hand. There are clear expectations for when the baby will sit, stand, walk, and be ready for toilet training. By contrast, the adolescent's unfolding is neither neatly organized according to a series of physiologic capabilities nor accomplished through interacting with two or three individuals. The teenager's needs are nothing less than the yearnings of humanity; the teenager interacts with an entire community.

In the early years, parents can control a child's environment. The child is limited by playpens, street crossings, the location of home and school. Parents can often decide to avoid certain situations, such as the interaction of their children with people of different values and backgrounds. As their children grow older, they are drawn into the larger community and are confronted with people and ideas that parents cannot control. The environment influences the child's experience in unpredictable ways, making it impossible to prepare for questions and conflicts the way you prepared both the child and yourself for her first day of nursery school.

Although you can talk in terms of what is not unusual for this period, it is more difficult to describe what is invariable. The upper-middle-class sixteen-year-old who already expects to go to college then to medical school will have an appreciably different experience from the one who dropped out of school two years ago and is living life on the streets. Their experience as teenagers has less in common now than their experience when they were both ten months old.

Where once there were right or wrong answers—"M" comes before "N" . . . wash your hands before eating . . . say "Thank you" for the present—now there are a series of judgment calls. What do you do when your fifteen-year-old buys a book on satanism? Do you confiscate it because you do not want him reading rubbish? If you confiscate it, are you saying that there is no freedom of speech/ideas in this house? What message are you giving if you abscond with your child's property, paid for with his allowance? Does the child's behavior indicate weirdness or a general interest in religious ideas? Is it a joke? A passing interest? Is it meant to rattle you? Is it a show of independence? Is the child reading the book because a friend recommended it? Should you read the book yourself so you can demonstrate that you take what the child does seriously? If you throw the book out, the issue will be resolved, or will it? Does the child need counseling? Should you ignore the entire episode?

This is a time when you fully confront what it means to live with ambiguities. You may be inclined to push your child to be cautious, so she can get through this period unscathed, but then you realize that not taking some risks can leave your child without much of a life. Do you urge being open to experience, or is it better to be safe rather than sorry? You want some balance but do not know how to accomplish that. Do you endorse different approaches at different times with a view to experimentation? Or should every option be systematically discussed in order to reach a "reasonable" opinion?

The child asks for something, and you say, "NO." He asks for something else, just a trifle less preposterous, and you say no again. The third time around, you still do not want to say yes, but you do so because you do not want to be seen as a naysayer and because this request is more reasonable than the other two. Suddenly, you realize that your child regularly uses this one-two-three approach in getting his way: Ask for the sun, moon, and stars in quick succession, and father will eventually give you a little sparkle as a consolation prize. You feel manipulated; you admire the child's cleverness. Are you proud, resentful, on guard, or all of the above?

The feelings generated are very complicated. Mother and daughter go to a movie and agree to eat afterwards. They return home after the show, and the child immediately flicks on the television. The mother feels cheated out of the promised dinner conversation and says so. The child says, "What's the big deal? I'm not hungry; we just spent an evening together, and there's something I want to watch on television." The mother feels that she is making a big deal out of a small incident, but that does not hold back the tears and the sense of having been set aside. The child does not understand what is going on, and neither does the mother. They are both annoyed with each other, and their vague disgruntlement serves the purpose of making sense out of the loosening of the ties that have bound them together.

It is not just your children's behavior with which you have to deal. Their friends are very important to them, and it is easy to feel jealous of these intimacies when your own relationship is full of awkward moments. When you see in her friend the behaviors that you disapprove of in your daughter, there is a tendency either to blame the friend for being a bad influence on your child or to comment freely about the friend's flaws. Not knowing your child's friend very well, you can use her as a representative of what is wrong with the younger generation: She does not have any manners . . . she just follows the crowd . . . she does not care about anything or any one. There may be an advantage in scapegoating the friend instead of your child, but there may be more advantage in regarding friends as an expression of your child's interests and asking her for help in understanding her friend: "You obviously like Amy. Tell me why you like her, so I can get to know her better." By taking your child's friends seriously, you demonstrate anew how much you care for her. By asking to understand her friends better, you may learn something new about how your child thinks.

While any given day may seem to last forever when there are arguments or strained silences, this transition decade is characterized by rapid changes. The child may begin these years unable to care for herself in key areas, and may end this decade responsible for a child of her own. The parents are left a bit breathless as they try to keep up with their child's enthusiasms and their own reactions to these shifts. The relationship between parent and child is being renegotiated, and that is bound to leave both generations feeling dislocated. Adjustments are not smooth but choppy. They take place in fits and starts, but the jerky, uncertain quality of the progress can be disquieting if not understood. That sense of being betwixt and between leaves parents feeling unsure of themselves, and when they are unsure of themselves they tend to revert back to controlling behaviors.

It is clear that adolescents need parenting which encourages autonomy, independence, curiosity, understanding, problem solving, and acceptance of individual differences. By contrast, parenting that impedes the child's development tends to be constraining, withholding, devaluing, judgmental, or excessively gratifying.[1] These statements are easier read than lived, because the preferred ways of relating often involve the parents' giving up past pleasures in favor of new, uncomfortable realities. For example, the woman who looked forward to having a daughter because she wanted to dress her in cute clothes and to decorate a nursery with frilly furniture and colorful animal characters may have some difficulty letting her teenager dress herself in uncute, punk clothes, rip off the old wallpaper, and hide the curlicued chest of drawers in the attic. The mother's loss of her loving and lovable baby may be more obvious to her than that the daughter is coming into her own. She has to come to appreciate that the daughter's wanting a room of her own is progress, not rejection.

It is easy to put the child's tastes down if they are raw and very different from your own. It is easy to be overindulgent if you still think the way you did in the early years, in terms of parents giving and children taking. It is easy to be withholding if you want to hold on to being *the* influence in your child's life. It is easy to be controlling if your own parents and friends continue to believe that you should be able to control your child and get him to do what you think is best. To avoid clinging to old parenting behaviors, you have to realize that moving your child forward involves replacing your old way of relating with more sophisticated notions. Your sense of accomplishment will not now come from clingingly cozy behaviors.

One of the paradoxes of this period is that the parents are being asked to validate the child's efforts to strike out on his own just when he is least likely to acknowledge directly what is best about them. The dynamics of this period call for a generosity in parents that few find easy to muster. It is not easy to be encouraging and facilitative when your child is telling you in many small ways that he no longer needs you; it is not easy to be affirming when you are rarely complimented for acting that way (though you are loudly criticized for not acting that way). The child needs his parents to value his developmental progress, but he is not likely to acknowledge their support in any obvious ways, for fear that applauding them will only reinforce their hold on him.

You would like to think that your child might say, "Dad, you really are good about letting me figure out what I want to do," but that compliment is unlikely to be delivered because the child is focusing on her struggle to find herself, not on how this is being facilitated by parents. She wants (and needs) to think that she is doing everything herself; she also may worry that any acknowledgment of being treated well will cause her parents to rest on their laurels and not exert themselves in future situations. This is a time when all parents identify with the mother who screamed out, "Do you notice that I am trying to be positively reinforcing of you? Well, I need some positive reinforcement from you, too. You need to remember to be kind to the nice mommy, so she can keep working hard on your behalf."

Parents frequently lament that their children take them for granted during this time. And it is true that the children want to be able to take their parents for granted. They want to think that their parents will always be there to come back to as they range far and wide. The child who cannot take her parents for granted is likely to be too insecure to be open to new experiences. Alas, being taken for granted makes the parents feel set aside or unappreciated when it should comfort them that their child is sure enough of her roots to presume on them. When parents want their children to be grateful for what they have received, they may be asking for something their children cannot give until they have moved away and have had an opportunity to look back.

The compliments of this period are indirect: "You should see how Jane's parents treat her; they tell her all the courses she should take and don't pay any attention to what she wants to do. If I had parents like that, I would say, 'Cut me open; take over my body; you obviously want to live my life for me.'" . . . "Boy, do John's parents lack taste! They pick paintings only on the basis of whether the orange shag rug has an orangy painting to go with it." . . . "Our family is really different; we talk at dinnertime. Jennifer's family is so boring. When they eat supper, all they say is, 'Pass the bowl of potatoes. Wasn't today cold?'" There is pride in family being expressed, but the direct compliment is likely to come when the child boasts of you to her friends, not to your face.

The goal of these years is for the child to explore brave, new worlds, while continuing to feel connected to his family. But the parent is bound to wonder whether the child will continue to feel connected, as he moves off in new directions. The inclination is to want to say to the child, "You can't have it both ways," yet that is exactly what adults want. They want to be separate individuals in a context of connectedness. Adult values are forged out of this tension between personal integrity and loyalty to family relationships, and this process gets under way during the teen years.

In a very real sense, the issue is, "Can the child have it both ways?" Will the parent shout, "Bon voyage," as the child explores worlds outside the family, and continue to be there for the child when she or he comes back to touch base? Too often parents think in terms of either/or: the child is either under their authority or is absolutely on his own. This is typified by the curse of some parents: "If you leave, don't come back." Parents get into this kind of mind-set because they are angry at the prospect of being discarded by the child. They feel rejected, even though what is being scrapped are dated ways of acting and relating, not themselves.

What are the dated ways of acting and relating that are being discarded? They include many of the practices that have been discussed in this book. The parent gives up the notion that she or he should be able to answer all of the child's questions and to save the child from making mistakes. The focus of parenting is not on possessiveness and manipulation of guilt, but on respect between the generations. Criticism is not viewed as just the prerogative of the parents, but children are entitled to their honest opinions. Accusations are expunged from the parenting repertoire. The assumption no longer is that children cannot solve their own problems; unsolicited advice is selectively offered. Where once the parent spoke for the child, now the child answers, without interruptions, when asked a question.

"Letting go" is the motif of this period, but it is a mistake to think that the emphasis is on letting go of the child. The letting go is of old ways of relating. The relationship is being transformed. In the first decade, the parents were concerned about providing their child with roots. In the second decade, the focus is on providing the child with wings, so she can be self-propelled. You may spend some time worrying about whether the roots are deep enough to retain equilibrium, but you cannot fret too much about that because it is the parents' confidence in the child's ability to be adequate to the tasks at hand that makes the wings grow strong.

Since the child's second decade is a transition between childhood and adulthood, its navigation is facilitated by appreciating where the parent-child relationship should be by its end. In

her book *Once My Child . . . Now My Friend,* Elinor Lenz
describes the goal as reaching a time when "all links of dependency with the child are dissolved, and the remaining ties are
those of friendship, sympathy, understanding, and acceptance
of each other's individuality."[2] For her, the critical test of the
parents' new way of relating is being ready to listen to their
children, and to act on their advice when it makes sense. This
is a view in which young adults and their parents are seen as
working together "toward symmetry and mutuality through
which they understand and treat each other as equals yet with
respect for their individual personalities."[3]

This is very different from the conventional view which holds
that the young person develops as an individual by moving
away from parents. Traditionally, the parents are not expected
to change much; the offspring do. Parents continue to act as
"parents," spouting a maxim on every occasion, while their
children seek to liberate themselves from the parent-child
bond. The children in this scenario are running away from the
parent of stand-up comedy: The father who argues with his
lawyer daughter, "Don't ask me *why;* the answer is NO." The
mother who says to her twenty-year-old son, "You only nag the
ones you love." The parent who asks grown children, "Does
anyone have to go to the bathroom before we leave?" What is
humorous is that the parent is an anachronism making comments that no longer apply. But these comedy staples are a serious reminder that parents can turn into jokes if they do not
change their ways of relating to their children.

It is not easy for parents to change their communication patterns. Parent-child interactions are frequently characterized
by the parents' imposing already-formed opinions onto their
children, but friendship tends to involve mutual understanding
rather than defending one's own position.[4] Parents are more
inclined to explain themselves than to try to understand their
child's vantage point. This sense of the parents' being entitled

to unilateral privileges may make it difficult for them to adopt the ground rules of friendship with the child: acceptance, openness, sympathy, self-revelation. You do not want a friend to tell you what to do as soon as you start talking about a problem. You want someone with whom you can feel comfortable and can share secrets of the heart.

The advantage for parents of aiming towards a reciprocal relationship, rather than one that is authority-based, is that this leaves parents more free to be themselves. There is a sense in which most parents conceal themselves from their children while they are growing up:

> We hastily broke off conversations when they entered the room, so they wouldn't catch us telling an off-color story or discussing the erotic passages of a best-selling book or exchanging anecdotes about our sexual experiences. We cleaned up our behavior in front of the children. We tried to keep our marital discord as well as our lovemaking out of their sight and hearing.[5]

In creating such a pasteurized environment, parents may have conveyed a false impression about themselves—that they are phony or boring. The more mutuality reigns, the more self-disclosure is permitted. The roles that individuals play as parent or child take second place to their relationship with each other.

I remember once listening to Cher speak about her mother on Phil Donahue's show. She said that when she was young her mother was everything to her. When she reached the age of fourteen, her mother became a lady who was always telling her things she did not want to hear. But during the adult years, her mother has become her best friend. That description, though oversimplified, captures some of the movement in parent-child relations over the decades. The parent, who was the center of the child's life in the early years, may be disregarded during the time when the child is seeking to become her own person, only to be appreciated, once she is on her own, as a special friend with whom she has so much in common.

Although the goal, as Elinor Lenz maintains, should be reciprocity between the generations, I disagree with her further belief that you only become a friend to your adult child in the process of becoming an *ex*-parent. Her conception of parenthood is that set of attitudes that characterizes roughly the first five years of parenthood: the controlling parent who responds best to dependency in the child. As the links of dependency are dissolved, Lenz thinks that you move to the stage of ex-parenthood, represented by friendship and acceptance of each other's individuality. Since her notion of parenthood is obsolete by the time the child reaches adulthood, she is forced to discard the role.

It makes more sense to acknowledge that you never stop being a parent, but that the nature of the role changes over time. By the second decade of parenthood, you are focusing less on meeting dependency needs and are assuming more of a responsive attitude in preparation for the time when mutuality will be totally the rule. The instrumental skills that are most effective when children are younger "work against the family when the children reach adolescence."[6] Those which are most effective with adolescents emphasize warmth, consideration, empathy, negotiation, and egalitarian decision-making. These qualities will prove vital in the development of reciprocal relations when parent and child come together as adults. There is indeed evidence to suggest that late adolescents already feel increasingly responsible for their parents and more loving as the parents' dominance decreases.[7]

To say that you become an ex-parent denies the distinctiveness of the relationship, which you do not have to repudiate in order to move forward. In a very real way, the parent represents the child's roots. To the extent that he always assumes that he knows where the child is coming from just because he is the father, he may listen less carefully to what is being said in the here and now. But knowing all that the child has been through can make him particularly understanding. Not only is there a shared background, but there may also be tastes and talents in common. The trick is to capitalize on the advantages conferred by the relationship without either taking the relationship for granted or requiring that it be hierarchical in structure.

Even though the relationship is no longer based on the dependency of childhood, the parent may also be special in that she or he can indulge the child when no one else thinks to do so. With Mom and Dad, the emerging adult may be able to collapse in a way that he cannot do elsewhere. The mother may give her daughter a check for a special treat when there is no particular occasion. The treats, of course, work both ways; the child may surprise Mother with a no-birthday present or cook a special dinner for Father. Such nurturing is a kindness born of friendship, so long as no price tag is attached—"I am buying your devotion." Indulgence that does not infantilize the recipient is one of the greatest gifts you can receive. It is an acknowledgment that the most competent people still need nurturing in order to get their batteries recharged. Parents who understand this are treasures who deserve nurturing in turn.

The last way in which parents remain special is that they never stop being models to their children. Ideally, they provide their children with a positive image of what life in the years ahead can be like. The eighteen-year-old learns something of what it means to be forty-six years old from his parent. Though other older friends can also serve this function, children are especially likely to use their parents' lives as the starting-off point for considerations of what they do and do not want to make of their lives. This aspect of the relationship continues up to the time when the child is witness to the parent's last days and learns from this death something more about her own mortality.

What do older children want from their parents? They do not want to be always in a one-down position vis-à-vis their parents—that is, parents always know best because they have lived longer. Children would like to be treated as if they were authorities in some areas just as their parents are masterful in others. This means that they do not want their experience to be regularly discounted—"Tired? You don't know what tired is; just wait till you get to be my age." . . . "Worried about a job, are you? What you're going through is nothing compared to the depression years I lived through." Children do not want parents to play one-upsmanship in order to feel whole themselves, but for each generation to listen to the other.

Children want their parents to see them as entitled to the same moods and emotions that they have. If parents can be peevish, spiteful, or anxious, then children should be allowed the same leeway. Not only can a child be pigheaded on occasion, but parents should not assume that any particular instance of behavior is prima facie evidence of character flaws (for which the only cure is nagging). Parents can have mean moments without being called mean, and so should their children.

Related to the right to feelings is the issue of whether children have to perform in a certain way in order to guarantee their parents' well-being. Children do not want to be weighed down by responsibility for their parents' feelings. There is something very uneven if parents feel that they have the right to share their griefs and expect sympathy, whereas children get told, "You will be the death of me," if they share any of their problems.

The question of whether the child can be honest about his feelings becomes a special issue when the child is away from home. If the emphasis is on the child's routinely assuring his parents that all is okay, then all mail will be like the camper who sends prewritten postcards weekly that only involve checking off set categories. If, instead, the emphasis is on communicating, then formula writing gives way to honest expression of feelings and perceptions.

Can a child write about real concerns without having to worry that a sermonette will come in the return mail, the point of which is the father's martyrdom on the cross of parenthood? One young woman remarked that she is forced to emphasize the positive in exchanges with her parents because they cannot take reality: "They want me to be always happy and to make them happy by living a fairy-tale life; I wish they would take responsibility for their own feelings. They can't find happiness in others, only in themselves." Some parents tend to blow their children's problems out of proportion because they feel so responsible for what happens to their children. The child's problem gets treated as a major failure because the parents feel like a failure if their child's life is anything but rosy and golden. What children want is to be responsible for their own lives and not to have their parents' crazy sense of omnipotence make any problems worse.

Most parents do want the child to "live happily ever after" because that means that they can stop feeling responsible (they continue to feel responsible long after they can actually do much to help). They therefore imagine some time when the child will be "settled." Traditionally, "settled" meant getting married. The parents would feel that they could now stop worrying about their child because a spouse was there to take over that function. "Settled" also meant finishing your education, getting a job with a sound pension plan, and buying a home to live in for the rest of your life. Now, marriages, educational requirements, job security, and affording a house are less certain than they once were. It has become more important, therefore, that parents not hold off treating their children as mature until they achieve stability in these areas. A young adult should be treated as grown up even if some parts of her or his life remain undecided; having some problems in these areas should not give parents a license to be intrusive. There is some tendency for parents to want their children to be settled, even if they themselves have never known an unruffled time.

Children want to be able to touch base with their parents regularly without having to worry that close contact will be regressive. When they are together, children do not want the conversation to dwell on the past. Reminiscing can be fun, but to the extent that parents identify their children with childish times, they make relations in the present difficult. The child feels like a disappointment for having grown up, which is not conducive to intimacy here and now.

One of the assumptions generally made by parents in the first two decades is that the child's "home" is where the parents are. Even when the child leaves home for the armed services, college, or a job in another city, the parents may expect the child to come back home to stay eventually. But every trip back may heighten that sense of not belonging there anymore. This may be especially true if the parents keep the child's room as a shrine to the past, for the child can see at a glance all the certificates, trophies, stuffed animals, and yearbooks that he has gone beyond. To the extent that parents and children see home-leaving differently there may be problems.[8] Home is the place where you feel secure, comfortable, and relaxed. Ironically, the child is most likely to feel "at home" with parents who recognize that their home may no longer be the child's home. And it is that sense of being "at home" with each other that is more important than place or possessions.

Being "at home" with each other means that relations are not stylized, crusted over with rituals that have to be practiced even when they have long lost meaning. Does the child have to be in place, performing certain functions, all day every Thanksgiving, Christmas, Passover, Mother's Day, Father's Day? Or can there be some variability? The more expectations are decreed like command performances, the less spontaneity there will be in the relationship. Children may be bodily present, but they may be aching to get away. They appreciate having parents acknowledge that they have the right to say what will work out for them in terms of scheduling.

Children generally feel responsible for their parents, particularly as they age.[9] But they have problems when their parents expect them to be available without any appreciation of how busy and complicated their lives are. It is not just parents who have obligations and pressures. To the extent that parents continue to think in terms of unilateral privileges, they may give orders rather than make requests, which causes the child's generosity of spirit to shrivel. Related to this is the problem of parents who are unwilling to articulate their needs, but expect the child to read their minds and meet their unspoken desires. For example, the mother who thinks that if her daughter truly loves her, she will know to buy her at Christmas the blue bathrobe that she has been wanting; or the father who expects his son to know, without being told, that he should call home from college every Sunday night. That kind of game playing is no substitute for open, honest conversation. And what the child wants in this situation, as well as all of the others that have been described, are the consideration and understanding of adult sharing.

For their part, parents do not want their children to spend their time together pouring over old grievances. That is not to say that a friendship-based relationship might not include some "When you did that, I felt _____." But children who dwell on the past are no more likely to develop intimate relations in the present than parents who have never gotten over the fact that their children grew up and contemplated leaving home. Hopefully, the child is able to see over time that the parents' weaknesses were more a function of context than of meanmindedness. For example, the father's unavailability was in part a function of having to commute long distances at a stretch. The mother's constant worrying about money was a result of her being left penniless with three small children on the death of her husband.

There was a limit to what the parent could do in that role because she or he was also a spouse, an employee, someone's child, a member of a community, someone's friend—all at the same time. Can the child understand the parent's perspective, not necessarily agreeing with that perspective but making the effort to empathize? Parents also ask that their past instances of obnoxious behavior be weighed less when they come together with their children than their overall patterns of caring. Hours of fussiness should not be noticed more than years of devotion.

Ideally, parents want a reciprocal relationship to develop so that neither party feels constrained by the other. There should not be that sense that the child will be able to live fully only when the parent is no longer around, or that the child cramps the parent's style. If there is a warm give-and-take, then parents may not have to worry as much about their later years. If the parent has stressed consideration and independence in relations with the child, then, hopefully, the child will be less inclined to seize on any eventual weakness in the parent as an opportunity to lord it over the parent. That means less likelihood of ugly role reversal—the child's wanting to play the domineering parent role to the older generation in order to get even. If the parent has always stressed mutuality, then the child will presumably do the same.

After this plea for mutuality, one caveat is in order: Parents should be prepared for the ambivalence their child will normally feel towards them. After you have tried to be the best parent that you knew how to be, it hurts to think that your child will have any feelings about you that are not super-positive, but *all* children do. Because parents have known their children during their most dependent time, there will always be some sense in which they will want to distance themselves (emotionally, geographically, or both) from their parents as they seek to become independent and effectual. The person who diapered you can always remind you of your vulnerability in a way that others cannot do—and some parents "tease" about the early years in a nasty way deliberately meant to "cut the child down to size." This need to distance themselves from their parents is greatest when children are panicked about whether they will ever come into their own (i.e., adolescence), but will continue so long as they feel that their parents do not really respect their rights and do not fully recognize their competence. Children often feel that they have to get away in order to return and be taken seriously. (Triumphant returns are a staple in the daydreams of children; the return of the prodigal son is an example of a return of mythic proportions.) After being with their parents for a few days, they will want to run away again if relations revert back to old patterns of fussing and fretting.

It is particularly difficult for parents, who have the best of intentions, to appreciate that even their child will feel some resentment towards them. They are likely to think that negative feelings make sense only if the child has been mistreated, and to get angry when their child seems so unappreciative of their efforts. But children can appreciate all of their parents' efforts and still worry about being swallowed up by their parents (their abilities, connections, resources, or problems). The parents' caring can easily come to symbolize their dependency, so children may withdraw from displays of concern as well as from chastisements. Because this is the case, mutuality and consideration between child and parent are doubly important. Otherwise, children will want to abscond and never want to return to parents who do not allow them to forget the foolish and raw parts of themselves. Can you be someone's child without being made to feel childish? is the question. Parents need to appreciate that these dynamics will operate even if they try their best to avoid any estrangement.

Tolerating their child's ambivalence towards them helps parents, in turn, better to tolerate their ambivalence towards the child. Even in the most loving situations, the parent is bound to feel some resentment when the child withdraws and seems unappreciative. Add to that the fact that even the most accomplished child will prove to be a disappointment in some way (e.g., the son is untidy; the daughter does not stand straight), and it is easy to see that parents will never feel only benevolent about their children. Indeed, this normal ambivalence serves the important purpose of making loosening the bonds easier. Picking at each other can serve a developmental purpose. The carping and tensions force both generations to consider whether they might not need to get away from each other for the general good. They both start wanting more personal space. The parents are ready to stop feeling responsible for what they can no longer control; the children are eager to be on their own.

The emphasis in this book has been on letting go of the ways of relating that characterized the first decade of parenthood in order to launch the child into society. More has been made of the sense of loss that flavors this period than of the sense of excitement, because it is always bittersweet when habits of belonging are forced to give way to a new order. The parent is bound to miss that sense of once having been "everything" to the child, especially if it has given way to wondering if you meant anything to the child. You may welcome the child's growing independence because it means release of sorts, but it is never easy to live through the process of fundamental change that precedes emancipation.

With the end of one era, however, a new one begins. When parent and child meet as adults enjoying each other's company, there is an opportunity for richness previously impossible to achieve. Even if relations during the teen years were difficult, it is exciting to know that once you have moved apart there is the possibility of coming together in ways yet uncharted. Freed of "oughts," new understandings are possible. There is something dialectical about this push-pull relationship: The child can react to parents' being "everything" by concluding that they have "nothing" in common, only to realize eventually that they are two special, complicated individuals who have "something very special" in common.

Parents learn much about themselves and life in the process of raising their children. One of the major areas of learning has to do with their relations to their own parents. Often there is a new sympathy that is now possible. To the extent that you went into adulthood resenting your parents for being overly demanding, this may be a time when you can appreciate that their pushing was meant to be encouraging and motivating, not harsh and derisive. Where once you focused only on their closed-mindedness and intolerance, now you can see where they were also open and supportive. Instead of blaming your father for his inability to talk about feelings, you can now appreciate how his traditional upbringing limited the development of those aspects of his personality. In wishing that your own children better understood your point of view, you may gain insights into your parents' perspective. You may also have some regrets when these insights come only after the death of a parent.

Ideally, you learn from raising your children something about the inevitability of struggle. Where once you might have expected that struggle could be avoided if you did or did not do certain things, you now realize that it is essential for development. Even after you have done your very best, your child will still have to struggle against you and what you believe in order to find herself. This unrest is not necessarily negative. Rebellion is not the privilege of any one generation; it is what all individuals have to do to some extent in order to find their own sense of identity. Parents have to realize that they can neither change nor avoid some things. As their children search for their special voices, their parents appreciate anew the old prayer for serenity: "Grant me the serenity to accept what I cannot change, the courage to change what I can, and the wisdom to know the difference between the two."

Learning to live with ambiguities is another important lesson that may have been learned. To the extent that you have learned to live with your child's strengths and weaknesses, and your own unevenness as a parent, you have gone beyond simplistic either/or thinking. The old notion that people are good or bad or that there is a right or wrong response for every occasion has given way to an appreciation that many situations are incapable of easy resolution. It takes time for some issues to become clear. Trying to understand dilemmas may be ultimately more important than resolving them. Development of any sort is not smooth; plateaus are only pauses on the way to the next set of questions. Realizing this, you have a tolerance for ambiguities which prevents premature closure. To the extent that you have learned to be satisfied as a good-enough parent with good-enough children and have given up expecting perfection, you have a sense of accomplishment that can be energizing.

Once the children are launched, parents have open to them new opportunities for personal growth. Some of the wonder of this period has been captured best in fiction. The heroine of Marge Piercy's *Fly Away Home*, as the title suggests, discovers a new sense of "home" after her two daughters are on their own—an augmented sense of sexual fulfillment, nurturance, friendship, commitment, and community.[10] The more she develops her own potential, the better her relationship with her children is. They cease to be the center of her life, and her newfound interests intrigue them now that she is less fixed on them; they begin to spend more time with her because she is an interesting person. The Amanda Cross mystery, *Sweet Death, Kind Death*, focuses on a professor with the conviction that middle age can be the greatest time of life. She changes the lives of those she touches; she sees middle age as an opportunity to be bold: ". . . to be free to sail, not to worry about living, to worry about living without adventure."[11] After you have done one of the major things that society expected of you (i.e., rearing children), there is a sense in which you can be free to be different, to be adventuresome.

There is relief when the last PTA meeting has drawn to a close. You no longer have to orchestrate the lives of several people, for they now can make their own plans. You have more time for yourself. Whether you see your life opening up or constricting will depend upon your attitude to the world. Do you fret and worry, overwhelmed by guilt, regrets, and recriminations, as this period comes to an end? Or do you take pleasure in all that you have accomplished, given limitations of all sorts? If you can take pleasure in your effort, chances are you can take pleasure in your child. You are not perfect—neither is the child—but there is a basic sense of satisfaction.

Raising children in a difficult world is a major accomplishment. It demonstrates an ability both to take risks and to give of yourself, of which you can be justifiably proud. Even if the experience did not work out as you once expected it would, you have learned much about how to handle frustrations, how to receive in giving and give in receiving. You have learned that helping someone come into her or his own does not mean that you lose face. In reading fables to your child, you have learned the various morals. In caressing away fears, some of your own nightmare thoughts have faded. In tolerating her off days, your own shortcomings matter less. In giving him space, you have opened up yourself.

Parenting is not the same as professional counseling, but, at their best, they both have in common helping the person realize that she or he has options and preparing the person to fly away. The second decade of parenthood is spent largely making sure that the child hones her decision-making skills and helping the child feel whole enough to set forth on her own. It is difficult to let go without there being strings attached—ties of guilt and gratitude to bind the child close. But as with so many things in life, acting one way can cause the opposite of what you expect. Tie the child to you, and the child will either run away or turn into a stone. Give the child wings, and the child will use them to fly back to you. We look to our children to provide meaning in our lives, only to reappreciate that we are the ones who have to provide meaning for ourselves.

I think the best way to end this book is to share my own thoughts and feelings on the occasion of my first child's turning eighteen two weeks after her high school graduation. I wanted to give her something memorable, because reaching voting age is a special birthday. It occurred to me that I had been collecting report cards, newspaper clippings, programs, and photographs over the years in large "achievement" boxes. I decided to get them out and to put together a scrapbook for her.

I was frustrated, as one might imagine, that I had not kept better track of dates and places. The years were a jumble out of which I had to make some order. The final product began with an invitation to our wedding and ended with photographs of her senior prom and graduation. In between were the hospital bill from when she was born, preschool drawings, class pictures, and photographs of those dear to her. I had been in charge of her life, and now I was putting a "this is your life"

album together. It pained me to part with some treasures—
the measuring tape describing how long she was at birth, the
newspaper clipping detailing spelling bee success at the re-
gional level. On the other hand, this was her life.

I gave her what had been in my safekeeping. She was now in
charge of her past—and her future.

• NOTES •

INTRODUCTION

1. Landon Y. Jones. *Great Expectations: America and the Baby Boom Generation* (New York: Ballantine Books, 1980), p. 79.
2. Ann Beattie, "Summer People," *The New Yorker*, September 24, 1984, p. 46.

CHAPTER ONE: THE GROWTH AND DEVELOPMENT OF PARENTS

1. Simone de Beauvoir, *The Second Sex*, trans. and ed. H. M. Parshley (New York: Bantam Books, 1952), pp. 493–94.
2. Betty Friedan, *The Feminine Mystique* (New York: Dell, 1963), p. 293.
3. Betty Rollin, "Motherhood: Who Needs It?" *Look*, September 22, 1970, pp. 15–17.
4. Jane Lazarre, *The Mother Knot* (New York: Dell, 1976).
5. Adrienne Rich, *Of Woman Born: Motherhood as Experience and Institution* (New York: W. W. Norton, 1976).
6. Shirley L. Radl, *Mother's Day Is Over* (New York: Charterhouse, 1973), p. 228.

7. Rochelle Paul Wortis, "The Acceptance of the Concept of the Maternal Role by Behavioral Scientists: Its Effect on Women," *American Journal of Orthopsychiatry*, 41, 5 (October 1971), pp. 733–46.

8. Vivian Gornick, "Woman as Outsider," in *Woman in Sexist Society*, ed. Vivian Gornick and Barbara K. Moran (New York: New American Library, 1971), p. 138.

9. Michael E. Lamb, "Fathers and Child Development: An Integrative Overview," in *The Role of the Father in Child Development*, 2nd ed., ed. Michael E. Lamb (New York: John Wiley, 1981), p. 32.

10. David Steinberg, "Redefining Fatherhood: Notes After Six Months," in *The Future of the Family*, ed. Louise Kapp Howe (New York: Simon and Schuster, 1972), p. 377.

11. Pamela Daniels and Kathy Weingarten, *Sooner or Later: The Timing of Parenthood in Adult Lives* (New York: W. W. Norton, 1982), pp. 1, 5.

12. Louise Bates Ames, *Child Care and Development* (Philadelphia: J. B. Lippincott, 1970), p. 273.

13. Jessie Bernard, *The Future of Motherhood* (New York: Dial, 1974), p. 364.

14. Nancy Chodorow, *The Reproduction of Mothering: Psychoanalysis and the Sociology of Gender* (Berkeley, CA: University of California Press, 1978), p. 218.

15. Margaret Mead, *Blackberry Winter* (New York: William Morrow, 1972), p. 282.

16. Elizabeth Janeway, *Man's World, Woman's Place* (New York: William Morrow, 1971), p. 150.

17. Letty Cottin Pogrebin, "Motherhood," *Ms.*, May 1973, p. 97.

18. Richard Q. Bell, "Socialization Findings Reexamined," in *Child Effects on Adults*, ed. Richard Q. Bell and Lawrence V. Harper (Hillsdale, NJ: Lawrence Erlbaum, 1977), p. 54.

19. Barclay Martin, "Parent-Child Relations," in *Review of Child Development Research*, Vol. IV, ed. Frances Degen Horowitz (Chicago: University of Chicago Press, 1975), p. 463.

20. Peter de Vries, *The Tunnel of Love* (Boston: Little, Brown, 1954), p. 98.

21. Reuben Hill and Paul Mattessich, "Family Development Theory and Life-Span Development," in *Life-Span Development and Behavior*, Vol. II, ed. Paul B. Baltes and Orville G. Brim, Jr. (New York: Academic Press, 1979), p. 199.

22. David Gutmann, "Parenthood: A Key to the Comparative Study of the Life Cycle," in *Life-Span Developmental Psychology: Normative Life Crises*, ed. Nancy Datan and Leon H. Ginsberg (New York: Academic Press, 1975), p. 167. In the same volume, see also a critique of the parental imperative: Patricia A. Self, "The Further Evolution of the Parental Imperative," pp. 185–89.

23. Erik H. Erikson, *Childhood and Society* (New York: W. W. Norton, 1950), p. 231.

24. Mary Catherine Bateson, *With a Daughter's Eye: A Memoir of Margaret Mead and Gregory Bateson* (New York: William Morrow, 1984), p. 207. In this book, Bateson describes her mother's role in getting Erikson to have his developmental stages read upward.

25. Roger L. Gould, *Transformations: Growth and Change in Adult Life* (New York: Simon and Schuster, 1978).

26. Daniel J. Levinson and associates, *The Seasons of a Man's Life* (New York: Alfred A. Knopf, 1978).

27. George Vaillant, *Adaptation to Life* (Boston: Little, Brown, 1977).

28. Gail Sheehy, *Passages: Predictable Crises of Adult Life* (New York: E. P. Dutton, 1976).

29. Gail Sheehy, "Catch-30 and Other Predictable Crises of

Growing Up Adult," *New York* magazine, February 18, 1974, pp. 30–44.

30. Roger L. Gould, "The Phases of Adult Life: A Study in Developmental Psychology," *American Journal of Psychiatry*, 129, 5 (November 1972), p. 526.

31. Alice S. Rossi, "Aging and Parenthood in the Middle Years," in *Life-Span Development and Behavior*, Vol. III, ed. Paul B. Baltes and Orville G. Brim, Jr. (New York: Academic Press, 1980), p. 147.

32. Therese Benedek, "Parenthood During the Life Cycle," in *Parenthood: Its Psychology and Psychopathology*, ed. E. James Anthony and Therese Benedek (Boston: Little, Brown, 1970), p. 185.

33. Robert W. White, *Lives in Progress*, 3rd ed. (New York: Holt, Rinehart and Winston, 1975), p. 361.

34. Carol Boellhoff Giesen and Nancy Datan, "The Competent Older Woman," in *Transitions of Aging*, ed. Nancy Datan and Nancy Lohmann (New York: Academic Press, 1980), p. 65.

CHAPTER TWO: DREAMERS

1. David Elkind, *All Grown Up & No Place to Go* (Reading, MA: Addison-Wesley, 1984), pp. 4–5.

2. Paul Henry Mussen, John Janeway Conger, and Jerome Kagan, *Child Development and Personality*, 4th ed. (New York: Harper & Row, 1974), p. 556.

3. Peter Blos, *On Adolescence: A Psychoanalytic Interpretation* (New York: Free Press, 1962), p. 10.

4. Patricia Y. Miller and William Simon, "The Development of Sexuality in Adolescence," in *Handbook of Adolescent Psychology*, ed. Joseph Adelson (New York: John Wiley, 1980), p. 389.

5. Jerome Kagan, "The Psychological Requirements for Human Development," in *Family in Transition*, 4th ed., ed.

Arlene S. Skolnick and Jerome H. Skolnick (Boston: Little, Brown, 1983), p. 418.

6. Daniel P. Keating, "Thinking Processes in Adolescence," in *Handbook of Adolescent Psychology*, p. 212.

7. John Janeway Conger, "Parent-Child Relationships, Social Change and Adolescent Vulnerability," *Journal of Pediatric Psychology*, 2, 3 (1977), p. 94.

8. Raymond Montemayor, "The Relationship Between Parent-Adolescent Conflict and the Amount of Time Adolescents Spend Alone and with Parents and Peers," *Child Development*, 53, 6 (December 1982), pp. 1512–19.

CHAPTER THREE: ANXIETY DREAMS

1. E. James Anthony, "The Reactions of Parents to Adolescents and to Their Behavior," in *Parenthood: Its Psychology and Psychopathology*, ed. E. James Anthony and Therese Benedek (Boston: Little, Brown, 1970), p. 317.

2. George Vaillant, *Adaptation to Life* (Boston: Little, Brown, 1977), p. 336.

3. Lillian E. Troll, *Early and Middle Adulthood: The Best Is Yet to Be—Maybe* (Monterey, CA: Brooks/Cole, 1975), p. 30.

4. Robert C. Peck, "Psychological Developments in the Second Half of Life," in *Middle Age and Aging: A Reader in Social Psychology*, ed. Bernice L. Neugarten (Chicago: University of Chicago Press, 1968), pp. 88–90.

5. Bernice L. Neugarten, "The Awareness of Middle Age," in *Middle Age and Aging: A Reader in Social Psychology*, p. 97.

6. Daniel J. Levinson, "A Conception of Adult Development," *American Psychologist*, 41, 1 (January 1986), p. 5.

7. Joanne Sabol Stevenson, *Issues and Crises During Middlescence* (New York: Appleton-Century-Crofts, 1977), p. 18.

8. Daniel J. Levinson and associates, *The Seasons of a Man's Life* (New York: Alfred A. Knopf, 1978), p. 49.
9. Gail Sheehy, *Passages: Predictable Crises of Adult Life* (New York: E. P. Dutton, 1976), p. 261.
10. Jessie Bernard, *Women, Wives, Mothers: Values and Options* (Chicago: Aldine, 1975), p. 111.
11. Sheehy, *Passages*, p. 243.
12. Roger L. Gould, "The Phases of Adult Life: A Study in Developmental Psychology," *American Journal of Psychiatry*, 129, 5 (November 1972), p. 525.
13. Patricia Meyer Spacks, *The Adolescent Idea: Myths of Youth and the Adult Imagination* (New York: Basic Books, 1981), pp. 3–5.
14. *Ibid.*, p. 191.

CHAPTER FOUR: THE PHYSICAL WORK IS OVER, BUT . . .

1. Joan Aldous, *Family Careers: Developmental Change in Families* (New York: John Wiley, 1978), p. 84.
2. Saul L. Brown, "Functions, Tasks, and Stresses of Parenting: Implications for Guidance," in *Helping Parents Help Their Children*, ed. L. Eugene Arnold (New York: Brunner/Mazel, 1978), pp. 22–34.
3. Robert Selman, *The Development of Interpersonal Understanding* (New York: Academic Press, 1980), pp. 147–51.
4. Patricia Meyer Spacks, *The Adolescent Idea: Myths of Youth and the Adult Imagination* (New York: Basic Books, 1981), p. 68.
5. Eda J. LeShan, *How to Survive Parenthood* (New York: Random House, 1965), pp. 21–29.
6. *Ibid.*, p. 37.
7. Alice S. Rossi, "Aging and Parenthood in the Middle Years," in *Life-Span Development and Behavior*, Vol. III,

ed. Paul B. Baltes and Orville G. Brim, Jr. (New York: Academic Press, 1980), p. 192.

CHAPTER FIVE: SAVING YOUR CHILD FROM MAKING MISTAKES

1. Rhona Rapoport, Robert N. Rapoport, and Ziona Strelitz, *Fathers, Mothers and Society: Towards New Alliances* (New York: Basic Books, 1977), p. 281.
2. Byron W. Lindholm and John Touliatos, "Mothers' and Fathers' Perceptions of Their Children's Psychological Adjustment," *Journal of Genetic Psychology*, 139, 2 (December 1981), pp. 245–55.
3. Patricia Noller, "Cross-Gender Effect in Two-Child Families," *Developmental Psychology*, 16, 2 (March 1980), pp. 159–60.
4. Lois Leiderman Davitz and Joel Robert Davitz, *How to Live (Almost) Happily with a Teenager* (Minneapolis: Winston Press, 1982), p. 93.
5. Bruce W. Darby and Barry R. Schlenker, "Children's Reactions to Apologies," *Journal of Personality and Social Psychology*, 43, 4 (October 1982), p. 742.

CHAPTER SIX: ONE LAST SERMON

1. Glenn H. Elder, Jr., "Parental Power Legitimation and Its Effect on the Adolescent," *Sociometry*, 26, 1 (March 1963), p. 57. See also Catherine R. Cooper, Harold D. Grotevant, and Sherri M. Condon, "Individuality and Connectedness in the Family as a Context for Adolescent Identity Formation and Role-Taking Skill," in *Adolescent Development in the Family*, ed. Harold D. Grotevant and Catherine R. Cooper (San Francisco: Jossey-Bass, 1983), p. 56.
2. Norman A. Sprinthall and W. Andrew Collins, *Adolescent Psychology: A Developmental View* (Reading, MA: Addison-Wesley, 1984), pp. 234–35.

3. Cyrus S. Stewart and Mary M. Zaenglein-Senger, "The Parent-Adolescent Power Contest," *Social Casework: The Journal of Contemporary Social Work*, 63, 8 (October 1982), pp. 458–60.
4. Lois A. Weithorn and Susan B. Campbell, "The Competency of Children and Adolescents to Make Informed Treatment Decisions," *Child Development*, 53, 6 (December 1982), pp. 1589–98.
5. Diana Baumrind, "Early Socialization and Adolescent Competence," in *Adolescence in the Life Cycle: Psychological Change and Social Context*, ed. Sigmund E. Dragastin and Glen H. Elder, Jr. (Washington, DC: Hemisphere Publishing, 1975), pp. 117–43. See also Herbert Yahraes, "Diana Baumrind. Parents as Leaders: The Role of Control and Discipline," in *Families Today*, Vol. I, ed. Eunice Corfman (Washington, DC: U.S. Government Printing Office, 1979), pp. 289–97.

CHAPTER SEVEN: A TASTE FOR VENGEANCE

1. Craig A. Smith and Phoebe C. Ellsworth, "Patterns of Cognitive Appraisal in Emotion," *Journal of Personality and Social Psychology*, 48, 4 (April 1985), pp. 813–38.
2. Harold H. Kelley and John L. Michela, "Attribution Theory and Research," in *Annual Review of Psychology*, Vol. XXXI, ed. Mark R. Rosenzweig and Lyman W. Porter (Palo Alto, CA: Annual Reviews, 1980), pp. 457–501.
3. David Burns, *Feeling Good: The New Mood Therapy* (New York: William Morrow, 1980). This book describes how depression is linked to distortions in thinking.
4. David H. Olson, Hamilton I. McCubbin, and associates, *Families: What Makes Them Work?* (Beverly Hills, CA: Sage Publications, 1983), p. 220.
5. Sally Van Zandt and Mary Louise DeHaan, "Adolescent

Daughters' Perceptions of Their Mothers," in *Family Strengths: Roots of Well-Being*, ed. Nick Stinnett, John DeFrain, Kay King, Patricia Knaub, and George Rowe (Lincoln: University of Nebraska Press, 1981), p. 335.

6. David Elkind, *All Grown Up & No Place to Go* (Reading, MA: Addison-Wesley, 1984), p. 203.

7. Kenneth G. Terkelsen, "Toward a Theory of the Family Life Cycle," in *The Family Life Cycle: A Framework for Family Therapy*, ed. Elizabeth A. Carter and Monica McGoldrick (New York: Gardner Press/John Wiley, 1980), p. 33.

CHAPTER EIGHT: ROOTS AND WINGS

1. Stuart T. Hauser, Sally I. Powers, Gil G. Noam, Alan M. Jacobson, Bedonna Weiss, and Donna J. Follansbee, "Familial Contexts of Adolescent Ego Development," in *Child Development*, 55, 1 (February 1984), pp. 195–213.

2. Elinor Lenz, *Once My Child . . . Now My Friend* (New York: Warner Books, 1981), p. 3.

3. James Youniss, "Social Construction of Adolescence by Adolescents and Parents," in *Adolescent Development in the Family*, ed. Harold D. Grotevant and Catherine R. Cooper (San Francisco: Jossey-Bass, 1983), p. 97.

4. Fumiyo Tao Hunter, "Adolescents' Perception of Discussions with Parents and Friends," *Developmental Psychology*, 21, 3 (May 1985), pp. 433–40.

5. Lenz, *op. cit.*, p. 65.

6. James F. Alexander, Joan Coles, and R. Steven Schiavo, "Parents as Leaders of Adolescents: A Developmental Model," in *Family Strengths: Continuity and Diversity*, ed. George Rowe, John DeFrain, Herbert Lingren, Ruth MacDonald, Nick Stinnett, Sally Van Zandt, and Rosanne Williams (Newton, MA: Education Development Center, Inc., 1984), p. 169.

7. Sandra Pipp, Phillip Shaver, Sybillyn Jennings, Susie Lamborn, and Kurt W. Fischer, "Adolescents' Theories About the Development of Their Relationships with Parents," *Journal of Personality and Social Psychology*, 48, 4 (April 1985), p. 1000.

8. DeWayne Moore, "Parent-Adolescent Separation: Intrafamilial Perceptions and Difficulty Separating from Parents," *Personality and Social Psychology Bulletin*, 10, 4 (December 1984), pp. 611–19.

9. Carol Austin Bridgewater, "Unselfish Baby Boomers," *Psychology Today*, April 1985, p. 14.

10. Marge Piercy, *Fly Away Home* (New York: Fawcett Books, 1984).

11. Amanda Cross, *Sweet Death, Kind Death* (New York: Ballantine Books, 1984), p. 97.

• BIBLIOGRAPHY •

Adams, G. R., and Gullotta, T. (1983). *Adolescent Life Experiences*. Monterey, CA: Brooks/Cole.

Adelson, J., ed. (1980). *Handbook of Adolescent Psychology*. New York: John Wiley.

Aldous, J. (1978). *Family Careers: Developmental Change in Families*. New York: John Wiley.

Aldrich, C. K. (1974). "Youth's Fulfillment of Adult Prophecies," *Australian and New Zealand Journal of Psychiatry*, 8: 127–29.

Allen, V. L., and Van de Vliert, E., eds. (1982). *Role Transitions: Explorations and Explanations*. New York: Plenum Press.

Alpert, J. L., and Richardson, M. S. (1980). "Parenting," in L. W. Poon, ed., *Aging in the 1980s: Psychological Issues*. Washington, DC: American Psychological Association, pp. 441–54.

Anthony, E. J., and Benedek, T., eds. (1970). *Parenthood: Its Psychology and Psychopathology*. Boston: Little, Brown.

Arnold, L. E., ed. (1978). *Helping Parents Help Their Children*. New York: Brunner/Mazel.

Bakan, D. (1966). *The Duality of Human Existence*. Chicago: Rand McNally.

Barber, V., and Maguire, M. S. (1975). *The Mother Person*. New York: Bobbs-Merrill.

Barnett, R. C., and Baruch, G. K. (1978). "Women in the Middle Years," *Psychology of Women Quarterly*, 3: 187–97.

Bartz, K. W. (1978). "Selected Childrearing Tasks and Problems of Mothers and Fathers," *The Family Coordinator*, 27: 209–14.

Baruch, G. K., and Barnett, R. (1986). "Role Quality, Multiple Role Involvement, and Psychological Well-Being in Midlife Women," *Journal of Personality and Social Psychology*, 51: 578–85.

Bell, L. G., and Bell, D. C. (1982). "Family Climate and the Role of the Female Adolescent: Determinants of Adolescent Functioning," *Family Relations*, 31: 519–27.

Bell, R. Q., and Chapman, M. (1986). "Child Effects in Studies Using Experimental or Brief Longitudinal Approaches to Socialization," *Developmental Psychology*, 22: 595–603.

Bell, R. Q., and Harper, L. V., eds. (1977). *Child Effects on Adults*. Hillsdale, NJ: Lawrence Erlbaum.

Belle, D., ed. (1982). *Lives in Stress: Psychological Theory and Women's Development*. Boston: Sage Publications.

Belsky, J., Lang, M., and Huston, T. L. (1986). "Sex Typing and Division of Labor as Determinants of Marital Change Across the Transition to Parenthood," *Journal of Personality and Social Psychology*, 50: 517–22.

Bernard, J. (1974). *The Future of Motherhood*. New York: Dial.

———. (1975). *Women, Wives, Mothers: Values and Options*. Chicago: Aldine.

Berndt, T. J. (1982). "The Features and Effects of Friendship in Early Adolescence," *Child Development*, 53: 1447–60.

Black, S. M., and Hill, C. E. (1984). "The Psychological Well-Being of Women in Their Middle Years," *Psychology of Women Quarterly*, 8: 282–92.

Blos, P. (1962). *On Adolescence: A Psychoanalytic Interpretation.* New York: Free Press.

Brim, O. G., Jr., and Kagan, J., eds. (1980). *Constancy and Change in Human Development.* Cambridge, MA: Harvard University Press.

Brook, J., Whiteman, M., Gordon, A., Brenden, C., and Jinishian, A. (1980). "Relationship of Maternal and Adolescent Perceptions of Maternal Child-Rearing Practices," *Perceptual and Motor Skills*, 51: 1043–46.

Brown, B. B., and Lohr, M. J. (1987). "Peer-Group Affiliation and Adolescent Self-Esteem: An Integration of Ego-Identity and Symbolic-Interaction Theories," *Journal of Personality and Social Psychology*, 52: 47–55.

Buhler, C., and Massarik, F., eds. (1968). *The Course of Human Life: A Study of Goals in the Humanistic Perspective.* New York: Springer.

Burke, R. J., and Weir, T. (1979). "Helping Responses of Parents and Peers and Adolescent Well-Being," *The Journal of Psychology*, 102: 49–62.

Burns, D. (1980). *Feeling Good: The New Mood Therapy.* New York: William Morrow.

Chodorow, N. (1978). *The Reproduction of Mothering: Psychoanalysis and the Sociology of Gender.* Berkeley, CA: University of California Press.

Collins, W. A., ed. (1984). *Development During Middle Childhood: The Years from Six to Twelve.* Washington, DC: National Academy Press.

Committee on Public Education. (1973). *The Joys and Sorrows of Parenthood.* New York: Group for the Advancement of Psychiatry.

Conger, J. J. (1977). "Parent-Child Relationships, Social

Change and Adolescent Vulnerability," *Journal of Pediatric Psychology*, 2: 93–97.

———. (1981). "Freedom and Commitment: Families, Youth, and Social Change," *American Psychologist*, 36: 1475–84.

Corfman, E., ed. (1979). *Families Today*, Vol. I. Washington, DC: U.S. Government Printing Office.

Cowan, C. P., Cowan, P. A., Heming, G., Garrett, E., Coysh, W. S., Curtis-Boles, H., and Boles, A. J., III. (1985). "Transitions to Parenthood: His, Hers, and Theirs," *Journal of Family Issues*, 6: 451–81.

Cox, M. J., Owen, M. T., Lewis, J. M., Riedel, C., Scalf-McIver, L., and Suster, A. (1985). "Intergenerational Influences on the Parent-Child Relationship in the Transition to Parenthood," *Journal of Family Issues*, 6: 543–64.

Daley, E. A. (1977). *Father Feelings*. New York: Pocket Books.

Daniels, P., and Weingarten, K. (1982). *Sooner or Later: The Timing of Parenthood in Adult Lives*. New York: W. W. Norton.

Darby, B. W., and Schlenker, B. R. (1982). "Children's Reactions to Apologies," *Journal of Personality and Social Psychology*, 43: 742–53.

Datan, N., and Ginsberg, L. H., eds. (1975). *Life-Span Developmental Psychology: Normative Life Crises*. New York: Academic Press.

Davitz, L. L., and Davitz, J. R. (1982). *How to Live (Almost) Happily with a Teenager*. Minneapolis: Winston Press.

De Beauvoir, S. (1952). *The Second Sex*. Trans. and ed. H. M. Parshley. New York: Bantam Books.

Deutsch, H. (1944). *The Psychology of Women*, Vol. I. New York: Bantam Books.

Dodson, F. (1974). *How to Father*. Los Angeles: Nash.

Dragastin, S. E., and Elder, G. H., Jr., eds. (1975). *Adolescence in the Life Cycle: Psychological Change and Social Context*. Washington, DC: Hemisphere Publishing.

Elkind, D. (1981). *The Hurried Child: Growing Up Too Fast Too Soon*. Reading, MA: Addison-Wesley.

———. (1984). *All Grown Up & No Place to Go*. Reading, MA: Addison-Wesley.

Erikson, E. H. (1950). *Childhood and Society*. New York: W. W. Norton.

———, ed. (1978). *Adulthood*. New York: W. W. Norton.

Fein, R. A. (1976). "Men's Entrance to Parenthood," *The Family Coordinator*, 25: 341–48.

Freud, A. (1946). *The Ego and the Mechanisms of Defense*. Trans. C. Baines. New York: International Universities Press.

Friedan, B. (1963). *The Feminine Mystique*. New York: Dell.

Friedman, R. (1975). "The Vicissitudes of Adolescent Development and What It Activates in Adults," *Adolescence*, 10: 520–26.

Galdston, R. (1975). "The Rise of Youth Culture and the Decline of Parenthood," *Psychiatric Annals*, 5: 502–6.

Galinsky, E. (1981). *Between Generations: The Six Stages of Parenthood*. New York: Times Books.

Garbarino, J. (1982). *Children and Families in the Social Environment*. New York: Aldine.

Gecas, V., Calonico, J. M., and Thomas, D. L. (1974). "The Development of Self-Concept in the Child: Mirror Theory Versus Model Theory," *Journal of Social Psychology*, 92: 67–76.

Gecas, V., and Schwalbe, M. L. (1986). "Parental Behavior and Adolescent Self-Esteem," *Journal of Marriage and the Family*, 48: 37–46.

Gerson, M. (1986). "The Prospect of Parenthood for Women and Men," *Psychology of Women Quarterly*, 10: 49–62.

Gerson, M., Alpert, J. L., and Richardson, M. S. (1984). "Mothering: The View from Psychological Research,"

Signs: Journal of Women in Culture and Society, 9: 434–53.

Giele, J. Z., ed. (1982). *Women in the Middle Years.* New York: John Wiley.

Giesen, C. B., and Datan, N. (1980). "The Competent Older Woman," in N. Datan and N. Lohmann, eds., *Transitions of Aging.* New York: Academic Press, pp. 57–72.

Gilligan, C. (1982). *In a Different Voice: Psychological Theory and Women's Develpment.* Boston: Harvard University Press.

Gjerde, P. F. (1986). "The Interpersonal Structure of Family Interaction Settings: Parent-Adolescent Relations in Dyads and Triads," *Developmental Psychology,* 22: 297–304.

Gould, R. L. (1972). "The Phases of Adult Life: A Study in Developmental Psychology," *American Journal of Psychiatry,* 129: 521–31.

———. (1978). *Transformations: Growth and Change in Adult Life.* New York: Simon and Schuster.

Grotevant, H. D., and Cooper, C. R., eds. (1983). *Adolescent Development in the Family.* San Francisco: Jossey-Bass.

Hamilton, L. (1977). *Father's Influence on Children.* Chicago: Nelson-Hall.

Hareven, T. K., ed. (1978). *Transitions: The Family and the Life Course in Historical Perspective.* New York: Academic Press.

Harevan, T. K., and Adams, K. J., eds. (1982). *Aging and Life Course Transitions: An Interdisciplinary Perspective.* New York: Guilford Press.

Harris, I. D., and Howard, K. I. (1979). "Phenomenological Correlates of Perceived Quality of Parenting: A Questionnaire Study of High School Students," *Journal of Youth and Adolescence,* 8: 171–80.

———. (1981). "Perceived Parental Authority: Reasonable and

Unreasonable," *Journal of Youth and Adolescence,* 10: 273–84.

Harris, R. L., Ellicott, A. M., and Holmes, D. S. (1986). "The Timing of Psychosocial Transitions and Changes in Women's Lives: An Examination of Women Aged 45 to 60," *Journal of Personality and Social Psychology,* 51: 409–16.

Hauser, S. T., Powers, S. I., Noam, G. G., Jacobson, A. M., Weiss, B., and Follansbee, D. J. (1984). "Familial Contexts of Adolescent Ego Development," *Child Development,* 55: 195–213.

Hetherington, E. M., Cox, M., and Cox, R. (1976). "Divorced Fathers," *The Family Coordinator,* 25: 417–28.

Hill, M. (1973). *Parents and Teenagers.* New York: Public Affairs Pamphlets.

Hill, R., and Mattessich, P. (1979). "Family Development Theory and Life-Span Development," in P. B. Baltes and O. G. Brim, Jr., eds. *Life-Span Development and Behavior,* Vol. II. New York: Academic Press, pp. 161–202.

Hoffman, L. W. (1975). "The Value of Children to Parents and the Decrease in Family Size," *Proceedings of the American Philosophical Society,* 119: 430–38.

Howe, L. K., ed. (1972). *The Future of the Family.* New York: Simon and Schuster.

Hunt, D. G. (1974). "Parental Permissiveness as Perceived by the Offspring and the Degree of Marijuana Usage Among Offspring," *Human Relations,* 27: 267–85.

Hunter, F. T. (1984). "Socializing Procedures in Parent-Child and Friendship Relations During Adolescence," *Developmental Psychology,* 20: 1092–99.

———. (1985). "Adolescents' Perception of Discussions with Parents and Friends," *Developmental Psychology,* 21: 433–40.

Hunter, F. T., and Youniss, J. (1982). "Changes in Functions of

Three Relations During Adolescence," *Developmental Psychology*, 18: 806–11.

Jacobs, R. H. (1979). *Life After Youth: Female, Forty—What Next?* Boston: Beacon Press.

Janeway, E. (1971). *Man's World, Woman's Place.* New York: William Morrow.

Jessop, D. J. (1981). "Family Relationships as Viewed by Parents and Adolescents: A Specification," *Journal of Marriage and the Family*, 43: 95–106.

Jones, L. Y. (1980). *Great Expectations: America and the Baby Boom Generation.* New York: Ballantine Books.

Kelley, H. H., and Michela, J. L. (1980). "Attribution Theory and Research," *Annual Review of Psychology*, 31: 457–501.

Kessler, R. C., and McLeod, J. D. (1984). "Sex Differences in Vulnerability to Undesirable Life Events," *American Sociological Review*, 49: 620–31.

King, M. (1979). "Parental Self-Actualization and Children's Self-Concept," *Psychological Reports*, 44: 80–82.

Knaub, P. K. (1986). "Growing Up in a Dual-Career Family: The Children's Perceptions," *Family Relations*, 35: 431–37.

Kohl, H. (1978). *Growing with Your Children.* Boston: Little, Brown.

Lamb, M. E., ed. (1981). *The Role of the Father in Child Development*, 2nd ed. New York: John Wiley.

———. (1982). *Nontraditional Families: Parenting and Child Development.* Hillsdale, NJ: Lawrence Erlbaum.

Lazarre, J. (1976). *The Mother Knot.* New York: Dell.

Lenz, E. (1981). *Once My Child . . . Now My Friend.* New York: Warner Books.

Lerner, R. M., and Spanier, G. B., eds. (1978). *Child Influences on Marital and Family Interaction.* New York: Academic Press.

LeShan, E. J. (1965). *How to Survive Parenthood*. New York: Random House.

———. (1975). *The Wonderful Crisis of Middle Age*. New York: Warner Paperback Library.

Levine, J. (1976). *And Who Will Raise the Children? New Options for Fathers and Mothers*. Philadelphia: J. B. Lippincott.

Levinson, D. J. (1986). "A Conception of Adult Development," *American Psychologist*, 41: 3–13.

Levinson, D. J., Darrow, C. N., Klein, E. B., Levinson, M. H., and McKee, B. (1978). *The Seasons of a Man's Life*. New York: Alfred A. Knopf.

Lewis, R. A., Freneau, P. J., and Roberts, C. L. (1979). "Fathers and the Postparental Transition," *The Family Coordinator*, 28: 514–20.

Lindholm, B. W., and Touliatos, J. (1981). "Mothers' and Fathers' Perceptions of Their Children's Psychological Adjustment," *Journal of Genetic Psychology*, 139: 245–55.

Livson, F. B. (1976). "Patterns of Personality Development in Middle-Aged Women: A Longitudinal Study," *International Journal of Aging and Human Development*, 7: 107–15.

Loevinger, J. (1976). *Ego Development: Conceptions and Theories*. San Francisco: Jossey-Bass.

Lowenthal, M. F., Thurnher, M., and Chiriboga, D. (1975). *Four Stages of Life*. San Francisco: Jossey-Bass.

Lynn, D. B. (1974). *The Father: His Role in Child Development*. Monterey, CA: Brooks/Cole.

MacKinnon, C. A. (1982). "Feminism, Marxism, Methods, and the State," *Signs: Journal of Women in Culture and Society*, 7: 515–44.

Margolis, M. L. (1984). *Mothers and Such*. Berkeley, CA: University of California Press.

Martin, B. (1975). "Parent-Child Relations," in F. D. Horowitz, ed., *Review of Child Development Research*, Vol. IV. Chicago: University of Chicago Press, pp. 463–540.

McAdams, D. P., Ruetzel, K., and Foley, J. M. (1986). "Complexity and Generativity at Mid-Life: Relations Among Social Motives, Ego Development, and Adults' Plans for the Future," *Journal of Personality and Social Psychology*, 50: 800–7.

McBride, A. B. (1973). *The Growth and Development of Mothers*. New York: Harper & Row.

———. (1976). *Living with Contradictions: A Married Feminist*. New York: Harper Colophon Books.

———. (1984). "The Experience of Being a Parent," *Annual Review of Nursing Research*, 2: 63–81.

———. (1985). "Differences in Women's and Men's Thinking About Parent-Child Interactions," *Research in Nursing and Health*, 8: 389–96.

McBride, A. B., and McBride, W. L. (1981). "Theoretical Underpinnings for Women's Health," *Women and Health*, 6 (1/2): 37–55.

Miller, B. C., McCoy, J. K., Olson, T. D., and Wallace, C. M. (1986). "Parental Discipline and Control Attempts in Relation to Adolescent Sexual Attitudes and Behavior," *Journal of Marriage and the Family*, 48: 503–12.

Miller, J. B. (1976). *Toward a New Psychology of Women*. Boston: Beacon Press.

Mink, I. T., and Nihira, K. (1986). "Family Life-Styles and Child Behaviors: A Study of Direction of Effects," *Developmental Psychology*, 22: 610–16.

Montemayor, R. (1982). "The Relationship Between Parent-Adolescent Conflict and the Amount of Time Adolescents Spend Alone and with Parents and Peers," *Child Development*, 53: 1512–19.

Moore, D. (1984). "Parent-Adolescent Separation: Intrafamilial

Perceptions and Difficulty Separating from Parents," *Personality and Social Psychology Bulletin*, 10: 611–19.

Murray, A. D. (1979). "Infant Crying as an Elicitor of Parental Behavior: An Examination of Two Models," *Psychological Bulletin*, 86: 191–215.

Mussen, P. H., Conger, J. J., and Kagan, J. (1974). *Child Development and Personality*, 4th ed. New York: Harper & Row.

Muuss, R. E. (1975). *Theories of Adolescence*, 3rd ed. New York: Random House.

Neugarten, B. L., ed. (1968). *Middle Age and Aging: A Reader in Social Psychology*. Chicago: University of Chicago Press.

Noller, P. (1980). "Cross-Gender Effect in Two-Child Families," *Developmental Psychology*, 16: 159–60.

Notman, M. (1982). "Midlife Concerns of Women: Implications of the Menopause," in C. C. Nadelson and M. T. Notman, eds., *The Woman Patient: Concepts of Femininity and the Life Cycle*. New York: Plenum Press, pp. 135–44.

Nye, F. I., ed. (1982). *Family Relationships: Rewards and Costs*. Beverly Hills, CA: Sage Publications.

O'Donnell, L. (1982). "The Social World of Parents," *Marriage and Family Review*, 5: 9–36.

Offer, D., Ostrov, E., and Howard, K. I. (1982). "Family Perceptions of Adolescent Self-Image," *Journal of Youth and Adolescence*, 11: 281–91.

———, eds. (1986). *Patterns of Adolescent Self-Image*. San Francisco: Jossey-Bass.

Olson, D. H., and McCubbin, H. I. (1983). *Families: What Makes Them Work?* Beverly Hills, CA: Sage Publications.

Parke, R. D. (1981). *Fathers*. Cambridge, MA: Harvard University Press.

Peck, E. (1971). *The Baby Trap*. New York: Bernard Geis.

Pipp, S., Shaver, P., Jennings, S., Lamborn, S., and Fischer,

K. W. (1985). "Adolescents' Theories About the Development of Their Relationships with Parents," *Journal of Personality and Social Psychology*, 48: 991–1001.

Radl, S. L. (1973). *Mother's Day Is Over*. New York: Charterhouse.

Rallings, E. M. (1976). "The Special Role of Stepfather," *The Family Coordinator*, 25: 445–49.

Rapoport, R., Rapoport, R. N., and Strelitz, Z. (1977). *Fathers, Mothers and Society: Towards New Alliances*. New York: Basic Books.

Rich, A. (1976). *Of Woman Born: Motherhood as Experience and Institution*. New York: W. W. Norton.

Robertson, J. F. (1978). "Women in Midlife: Crises, Reverberations, and Support Networks," *The Family Coordinator*, 27: 375–82.

Rogers, V., ed. (1984). *Adult Development Through Relationships*. New York: Praeger.

Rossi, A. S. (1968). "Transition to Parenthood," *Journal of Marriage and Family*, 30: 26–34.

———. (1980). "Aging and Parenthood in the Middle Years," in P. B. Baltes and O. G. Brim, Jr., eds., *Life-Span Development and Behavior*, Vol. III. New York: Academic Press, pp. 138–205.

Rowe, G., DeFrain, J., Lingren, H., MacDonald, R., Stinnett, N., Van Zandt, S., and Williams, R., eds. (1984). *Family Strengths: Continuity and Diversity*. Newton, MA: Education Development Center, Inc.

Rypma, C. B. (1976). "The Biological Bases of the Paternal Response," *The Family Coordinator*, 25: 335–39.

Sangiuliano, I. (1980). *In Her Time*. New York: Morrow Quill Paperbacks.

Savin-Williams, R. C., and Small, S. A. (1986). "The Timing of Puberty and Its Relationship to Adolescent and Parent Perceptions of Family Interactions," *Developmental Psychology*, 22: 342–47.

Schaie, K. W., and Willis, S. L. (1986). "Can Decline in Adult Intellectual Functioning Be Reversed?" *Developmental Psychology*, 22: 223–32.

Sebald, H. (1986). "Adolescents' Shifting Orientation Toward Parents and Peers: A Curvilinear Trend over Recent Decades," *Journal of Marriage and the Family*, 48: 5–13.

Selman, R. (1980). *The Development of Interpersonal Understanding*. New York: Academic Press.

Sheehy, G. (1976). *Passages: Predictable Crises of Adult Life*. New York: E. P. Dutton.

Skolnick, A. S., and Skolnick, J. H., eds. (1983). *Family in Transition*, 4th ed. Boston: Little, Brown.

Smith, C. A., and Ellsworth, P. C. (1985). "Patterns of Cognitive Appraisal in Emotion," *Journal of Personality and Social Psychology*, 48: 813–38.

Smith, R. H., and Smith, A. R. (1976). "Attachment and Educational Investment of Adolescence," *Adolescence*, 11: 349–57.

Sorensen, R. C. (1974). "Adolescent Sexuality: Crucible for Generational Conflict," *Journal of Clinical Child Psychology*, 3 (3): 44–45.

Spacks, P. M. (1981). *The Adolescent Idea: Myths of Youth and the Adult Imagination*. New York: Basic Books.

Sprinthall, N. A., and Collins, W. A. (1984). *Adolescent Psychology: A Developmental View*. Reading, MA: Addison-Wesley.

Starr, B., and Weiner, M. B. (1981). *The Starr-Weiner Report on Sex and Sexualty in the Mature Years*. New York: Stein & Day.

Steinberg, L., and Silverberg, S. B. (1986). "The Vicissitudes of Autonomy in Early Adolescence," *Child Development*, 57: 841–51.

Steinberg, L. D. (1981). "Transformations in Family Relations at Puberty," *Developmental Psychology*, 17: 833–40.

———. (1987). "Single Parents, Stepparents, and the Susceptibility of Adolescents to Antisocial Peer Pressure," *Child Development*, 58: 269–75.

Stevens, J. H., Jr., and Matthews, M., eds. (1978). *Mother/Child Father/Child Relationships*. Washington, DC: National Association for the Education of Young Children.

Stevenson, J. S. (1977). *Issues and Crises During Middlescence*. New York: Appleton-Century-Crofts.

Stewart, A. J., Sokol, M., Healy, J. M., Jr., Chester, N. L., and Weinstock-Savoy, D. (1982). "Adaptation to Life Changes in Children and Adults," *Journal of Personality and Social Psychology*, 43: 1270–81.

Stewart, C. S., and Zaenglein-Senger, M. M. (1982). "The Parent-Adolescent Power Contest," *Social Casework: The Journal of Contemporary Social Work*, 63: 457–64.

Stinnett, N., DeFrain, J., King, K., Knaub, P., and Rowe, G., eds. (1981). *Family Strengths: Roots of Well-Being*. Lincoln: University of Nebraska.

Terkelsen, K. G. (1980). "Toward a Theory of the Family Life Cycle," in E. A. Carter and M. McGoldrick, eds., *The Family Life Cycle: A Framework for Family Therapy*. New York: Gardner Press/John Wiley, pp. 21–52.

Thomas, J. H. (1983). "The Influences of Sex, Birth Order, and Sex of Sibling on Parent-Adolescent Interaction," *Child Study Journal*, 13: 107–14.

Troll, L. E. (1975). *Early and Middle Adulthood: The Best Is Yet to Be—Maybe*. Monterey, CA: Brooks/Cole.

Vaillant, G. (1977). *Adaptation to Life*. Boston: Little, Brown.

Walters, J., and Stinnett, N. (1971). "Parent-Child Relationships: A Decade Review of Research," *Journal of Marriage and the Family*, 33: 71–111.

Walters, J., and Walters, L. H. (1980). "Parent-Child Relationships: A Review, 1970–1979," *Journal of Marriage and the Family,* 42: 807–22.

Waterman, A. S. (1982). "Identity Development from Adolescence to Adulthood: An Extension of Theory and a Review of Research," *Developmental Psychology,* 18: 341–58.

Weinberg, S. L., and Richardson, M. S. (1981). "Dimensions of Stress in Early Parenting," *Journal of Consulting and Clinical Psychology,* 49: 686–93.

Weithorn, L. A., and Campbell, S. B. (1982). "The Competency of Children and Adolescents to Make Informed Treatment Decisions," *Child Development,* 53: 1589–98.

White, R. W. (1975). *Lives in Progress,* 3rd ed. New York: Holt, Rinehart and Winston.

Wortis, R. P. (1971). "The Acceptance of the Concept of the Maternal Role by Behavioral Scientists: Its Effect on Women," *American Journal of Orthopsychiatry,* 41: 733–46.

Wright, P. H., and Keple, T. W. (1981). "Friends and Parents of a Sample of High School Juniors: An Exploratory Study of Relationship Intensity and Interpersonal Rewards," *Journal of Marriage and the Family,* 43: 559–70.

Youniss, J., and Smollar, J. (1985). *Adolescent Relations with Mothers, Fathers, and Friends.* Chicago: University of Chicago Press.

ABOUT THE AUTHOR

Angela Barron McBride received her bachelor's degree in nursing from Georgetown University, her master's degree in psychiatric/mental health nursing from Yale University, and her Ph.D. in developmental psychology from Purdue University. She is Professor and Associate Dean for Research, Development, and Resources at Indiana University School of Nursing. Dr. McBride is an Adjunct Professor both in the Department of Psychology at Purdue University School of Science in Indianapolis and in the Department of Psychiatry at Indiana University. Her work has been published in professional journals and popular magazines. She is the author of *The Growth and Development of Mothers* and *Living with Contradictions*.

INDEX